THE NAKED TRUTH

THE NAKED TRUTH
by Dave Simpson

JOSEF WEINBERGER PLAYS

LONDON

THE NAKED TRUTH
First published in 2015
by Josef Weinberger Ltd
12-14 Mortimer Street, London W1T 3JJ
www.josef-weinberger.com / plays@jwmail.co.uk

Copyright © 2015, 2008 by Dave Simpson
The author asserts his moral right to be identified as the author of the work.

ISBN: 978 0 85676 355 7

This play is protected by Copyright. According to Copyright Law, no public performance or reading of a protected play or part of that play may be given without prior authorization from Josef Weinberger Plays, as agent for the Copyright Owners.

From time to time it is necessary to restrict or even withdraw the rights of certain plays. It is therefore essential to check with us before making a commitment to produce a play.

NO PERFORMANCE MAY BE GIVEN WITHOUT A LICENCE

AMATEUR PRODUCTIONS
Royalties are due at least one calendar month prior to the first performance. A royalty quotation will be issued upon receipt of the following details:

Name of Licensee
Play Title
Place of Performance
Dates and Number of Performances
Audience Capacity and ticket price(s)

PROFESSIONAL PRODUCTIONS
All enquiries regarding professional rights should be addressed to Josef Weinberger Plays at the address above. Enquiries concerning all other rights should be addressed to the author/ c/o the publisher.

OVERSEAS PRODUCTIONS
Applications for productions overseas should be made to our local authorised agents. Further information can be found on our website or in our printed Catalogue of Plays.

CONDITIONS OF SALE
This book is sold subject to the condition that it shall not by way of trade or otherwise be re-sold, hired out, circulated or distributed without prior consent of the Publisher. **Reproduction of the text either in whole or part and by any means is strictly forbidden.**

Printed by Berforts Information Press Ltd, Stevenage

THE NAKED TRUTH was first presented by Theatre Productions Limited at the Forum Theatre, Billingham, on 27th May 2008 prior to a national UK tour. The cast was as follows:

TRISHA	Jo Farrell
BEV`	Lisa Riley
FAITH	Alison Young
SARAH	Pauline Fleming
RITA	Sarah White
GABBY	Paula Frances

Directed by Stephen Leatherland

CHARACTERS

Trisha. 24, attractive, slim, well dressed, immaculate.

Bev. 24, big, larger than life, outrageous.

Faith. 21, shy, mousey, naïve.

Sarah. late 40's, early 50's prim, proper, very moral.

Rita. 40, brassy, loud-mouthed, attractive but hard.

Gabby. 33, very fit, gorgeous, tough.

SET

All the action takes place in a village hall.

ACT ONE

Scene One

Lights up on a village hall. Music. Windows stage left and right, an entrance door and a door to the toilet. On the stage there are three poles erected on podiums. Lights up. GABBY *is doing an energetic warm-up exercise with* BEV, FAITH, TRISHA, SARAH *and* RITA. *The warm-up reveals each of their physical characteristics:* BEV, *loud and brash,* FAITH, *withdrawn, uncoordinated,* TRISHA, *very self-aware,* SARAH, *reticent, nervous,* RITA, *a go-for-it girl.*

GABBY	Hi, my name's Gabby, welcome to your first class. We're going to start with some exercises where you'll be stretching muscles you've not used since chapter eight of the Karma Sutra.
FAITH	Karma what?
	(*As they wobble their chest and move forward in the warm-up.*)
BEV	I can do this one.
	(*And as they repeat it* BEV *pushes out her ample chest.*)
	Suck 'em and see!
	(*As they do a horse-ride.*)
	Ye-haa!
	(*At the end of the comic warm-up . . .*)
GABBY	Ladies, this is going to be hard work – for you and for me.
	(*Lights out. Spot up on* GABBY.)

GABBY (*to audience*) That was six months ago when five ladies first walked into my class. I don't think any of them realised what they were getting into or how this was going to totally affect all their lives . . .

(*Spot out. Lights up on* BEV *and* FAITH. BEV *is large, over-weight and wearing a not very flattering, bright, pink, gaudy leotard. She's very made up, with an equally bright head-band. She is testing the pole as if thinking, "is this going to hold my weight?"* FAITH, *looking like a scared rabbit, wears a baggy t-short and huge shorts that are too big. She carries a plastic bag. As the lights come up she is staring at the Notice Board with a large poster advertising the Pole Dancing Classes.*)

FAITH Oh, it's pole dancing classes!

BEV Yeh, what the frigging heck did you think it was?

FAITH I don't know, I thought maybe it was laptop dancing classes.

BEV Laptop dancing!

FAITH Yeh.

BEV Could you see me dancing on a laptop?

(*She does a little demonstration.*)

FAITH Ohhh! Sorry. (*Pause. She's scared. Suddenly.*) I'm going home.

(*She grabs her bag, hurries to the exit, before* BEV *drags her back.*)

BEV Don't be a soft git. If I'm gonna dangle me wobbly bits from a friggin' pole, so are you!

FAITH	But Bev, I'm just not a sexual person like you.
BEV	Faith, are you happy with yourself?
FAITH	You know I'm not.
BEV	D'you want a fellah?
FAITH	Well I wouldn't say no.
BEV	That'll make you very popular.
FAITH	But it'd have to be the right man.
BEV	Faith, let's be honest, what you really need is a bloody good shag.
FAITH	Bev, please. All I really want . . .
BEV	. . . Is a meaningful relationship. I know, I know. Faith, take a tip from a sexpert . . . meaningful relationships only last as long as two minutes . . . the length of time it takes a fellah to come.
FAITH	Oh you're so cynical, Bev.
BEV	Cynical but successful. See a lot of people'd look at me and think, fat cow, bet she never gets laid . . .
FAITH	Oh they wouldn't say that.
BEV	But you see, Faith, I've learnt to use the assets I've got.
FAITH	And what are they?
BEV	Big ones, Faith, big ones!
FAITH	And what assets have I got?

BEV   (*beat*) You've a lovely personality.

FAITH   And? What else?

BEV   It's all down to confidence, Faith.

FAITH   So why don't fellahs fancy me?

BEV   You have to believe in yourself – and learn to love your body. Like I do. And once you've learnt that, the men'll come flocking.

FAITH   You think so?

BEV   They'll be lining up as if you're offering 'em a fish and chip supper and a dirty DVD.

FAITH   You think so?

BEV   I know so. And that's why you're not copping out now, I want to see you wrapping your thighs round that pole . . . as if it's a man.

FAITH   Oh God, no, oh I feel sick, I feel absolutely sick!

          (*She digs in her plastic bag as if she's getting a handkerchief because she feels ill, but instead takes out wrapped sandwiches.*)

FAITH   Would you like a cheese and marmalade sandwich?

BEV   I thought you were feeling sick!

FAITH   I'm always starving when I'm nervous. Just before me driving test I had a curry and when I did the emergency stop I was sick all over the steering wheel.

BEV	That's why I don't drink and drive – I kept spilling me pint all over me steering wheel.
	(*And* FAITH *starts munching on her sandwich as* TRISHA *enters. She looks very attractive in a designer exercise gear. She stops when she sees* BEV *and* FAITH.)
TRISHA	Oh, have I come to the wrong place?
BEV	I don't know, have you?
TRISHA	I was looking for the pole dancing classes . . . (*Looking* BEV *up and down.*) . . . but tonight it's Weight Watchers Club, yes?
BEV	No.
TRISHA	No?
BEV	Actually, you're looking at the future of pole dancing.
	(*And she wobbles her tits.*)
TRISHA	Sorry?
BEV	They're opening a new pole dancing club in town – it's called Fat Birds.
TRISHA	Really?
BEV	Have you not read about it in *GQ* and *Marie Claire*?
TRISHA	Read what?
BEV	Thin is out, fat is in.

TRISHA   No, I haven't read that.

BEV   Yeh, fat is the new thin.

TRISHA   You're joking, aren't you?

BEV   No, I'm serious. All the modelling agencies are now looking for women with big fat thighs, huge tits and bulging bellies.

              (TRISHA *looks confused.*)

              And in a recent *GQ* survey eighty percent of guys under thirty said they were now only looking to go with big, fat birds.

TRISHA   No!

BEV   They were requesting centrefolds of . . . Jo Brand, Dawn French and errr . . . Beth Ditto.

FAITH   She is joking. And yes this is where they're having the pole dancing classes.

TRISHA   Oh. Oh. And you two . . . (*Suddenly laughing as if understanding.*) . . . you're the cleaners, aren't you?

BEV   Hey and how would you like a mop stuck right up your thin, boney arse?!

FAITH   Bev! No, we're here for the pole dancing class as well. (*Placating* TRISHA *with a sandwich.*) Would you like a cheese and marmalade sandwich?

TRISHA   (*appalled at the thought*) Certainly not. (*Then looking at* BEV.) Just a minute, don't I know you?

BEV   Yeh, I think we slept together when you went through your lesbian period.

TRISHA	(*ignoring this*) No, I definitely do know you. Did you just say Bev?
FAITH	Yes, this is Bev and I'm Faith.
TRISHA	Hang on . . . it's Beverley Barker, isn't it?
FAITH	How did you know that?
TRISHA	(*to* BEV) I was at school with you.
BEV	I don't think so, love.
TRISHA	(*points to herself*) Trisha Morgan.
BEV	Trisha Morgan?
TRISHA	(*smiling*) Yes.
BEV	Trisha *Morgan*?!!
TRISHA	(*proud*) Yes.
BEV	You mean that big fat spotty kid who wet her pants 'cos the lads took the piss?
`	(*Beat.*)
TRISHA	I wasn't that spotty!
BEV	(*to* FAITH) Bloody hell, she's lost loads of weight.
TRISHA	You know up to two years ago I weighed thirteen stone.
FAITH	No!
TRISHA	Then I met Gareth and he changed my life.

FAITH	Oh. Who's Gareth?
TRISHA	My husband of ten months, two weeks and six days. He saw something in me no one else saw.
BEV	And he still married you?
TRISHA	(*ignoring this*) Behind the thirteen stone he saw the inner me. The slim, beautiful inner me. And from the moment I met him, I changed. By my wedding day I'd gone from a size sixteen to a ten.
FAITH	That's amazing.
TRISHA	I know. But you could do it, Bev.
BEV	Excuse me, I'm happy with my body.
TRISHA	How could you possibly be happy looking like . . .
BEV	. . . Watch it!
TRISHA	I mean I'm sorry, Bev, but . . . (*Gestures.*) . . . look at you. Every girl I know wants a slim figure. And every man I know wants a wife who's slim and attractive.
BEV	Nothing worse than a bloody convert.
TRISHA	Okay. Quick test. Are you married, Bev?
BEV	No . . .
TRISHA	Exactly!
BEV	. . . But take it from me, Trish, I know lots of men who like big women.
TRISHA	Maybe – as a novelty value.

Bev	You cheeky bitch!
Trisha	I'm only saying!
Bev	You really think guy's'd prefer your skinny little body to mine.
Trisha	(*smiling patronisingly*) No contest, darling.
Bev	Two minutes with you and a guy's explored every inch, with me it'd take two years!!

(Faith *splutters with laughter at* Trisha.)

In fact, most men I've been with, I have to give 'em directions how to get there.

(Faith *laughs again.*)

Down a bit, up a bit, to the side, nearly there . . . ohhh . . . ohhh!

(*As a nervous* Sarah *enters.*)

Sarah	Hi.

(*They all say 'hi'.*)

Is this the, er . . .

Bev	Pole dancing classes, yeh.
Trisha	I'm Trisha, this is Bev . . .
Faith	. . . And I'm Faith.
Sarah	Hello, I'm Sarah. (*They all say "Hi, Sarah".*) Well this is a relief.

TRISHA: What is?

SARAH: I was worried the class would be filled with eighteen year old wannabe pole-dancers with perfect bodies.

BEV: No, only me.

SARAH: I have to say I am a bit nervous about it all.

FAITH: Oh and me! Bev 'ere dragged me along, I didn't want to come. (*Quickly.*) Would you like a cheese and marmalade sandwich?

SARAH: No, thanks, I've already eaten.

TRISHA: (*looking* SARAH *up and down critically*) I take it you're not here because you want to be a pole dancer?

SARAH: (*laughing nervously*) Oh no.

TRISHA: Didn't think so at your age.

BEV: (*to* SARAH) Sorry, she's got a mouth bigger than my arse.

TRISHA: I'm only saying . . .

SARAH: That's okay.

TRISHA: So what are you doing here then?

SARAH: Well, I . . . I want to keep fit and, er . . .

TRISHA: And I suppose you've got to look after your weight now you've passed your prime . . .

BEV: Will you give it a rest!

FAITH	Well I think you've got a lovely figure anyway.
SARAH	(*smiles a 'thank you', then*) Mind you, it is one of life's mysteries, isn't it? . . . you hang a summer dress in your wardrobe and over the winter it's shrunk two sizes.
TRISHA	Yes. I'm actually going to have a boob job.
	(*And this takes them all by surprise.* SARAH *is particularly frosty throughout this exchange.*)
SARAH	Really?
TRISHA	I'd like to go from my current 34C to 34 double D.
SARAH	Why?
TRISH	What d'you mean, why?
SARAH	You've got perfectly good breasts, why do you want surgery?
TRISHA	I'll . . . well I'll be happier with a size 34 double D.
SARAH	You think bigger breasts will make you happier?
TRISHA	Yes. And they'd make Gareth happier. He's always liked big breasts.
BEV	Then let him have the operation, he can feel himself up.
TRISHA	(*ignoring this*) I've actually got a consultation with a plastic surgeon tomorrow.
FAITH	No! Is it because you want to be a professional pole dancer?

TRISHA   You must be joking! I wouldn't demean myself.

FAITH   So why d'you want to do pole dancing, Trisha?

TRISHA   (*smiles*) To give my Gareth a surprise. You see I'm a firm believer in keeping our sex life fresh and exciting and varied . . .

SARAH   (*cool*) Really?

TRISH   Oh yes. A happy man in the bed is a happy and devoted husband.

BEV   Thank you, Miriam Stoppard.

TRISHA   I think experimentation is the key to a fulfilling sexual marriage.

SARAH   Do you? That's very interesting.

TRISHA   I'm always dressing up for him . . .

FAITH   You mean when you go out together . . . ?

TRISHA   (*ignoring this*) He particularly likes my nurse's uniform.

FAITH   What hospital do you work in, Trisha?

BEV   Faith, you need to get out more.

TRISHA   . . . And he loves my traffic warden's uniform . . .

FAITH   (*as the penny drops*) Oh, I get it! You've got two jobs!

BEV   It's role play, Faith. She's pretending.

FAITH   Ohhh!

TRISHA	. . . And of course I possess a basque, stockings and suspenders . . . and crotchless panties . . .
FAITH	Crotchless panties?!
TRISHA	One of Gareth's favourites . . .
BEV	. . . I'm sure he looks very nice in them.
FAITH	Oh I couldn't wear crotchless knickers, could you, Sarah?
SARAH	No, I don't think it's my thing.
FAITH	Well they'd be so draughty, wouldn't they?
TRISHA	. . . And I also recently bought a rabbit . . .
	(SARAH and FAITH are looking at her open-mouthed.)
SARAH	A . . . a rabbit?
	(TRISHA nods.)
FAITH	Er, what do you do with a rabbit?
BEV	(sound of vibrator) Zzzzzzzzz.
FAITH	Ohhh.
TRISHA	But then I read the latest fad is to own your own pole. So I've ordered one for Gareth's birthday.
SARAH	For . . . for his birthday?
TRISHA	I think he's going to be very surprised.
BEV	I bet it's something he's always wanted.

FAITH	(*sincere*) That's all very well, Trisha . . . but how will you wrap it up?

(She looks at FAITH, *realise she's being serious, shakes her head in despair. They don't see* RITA *who's arrived and stands apart, taking this in.)*

TRISHA	Anyway, to answer your original question, Faith, no, I have no intention of becoming a professional pole dancer. Earning money from pushing your breasts and crotch into a man's face . . . well it's no better than prostitution!

(RITA *steps forward where they can see her.*)

RITA	You reckon? Well I can't wait for a guy to stuff tenners down me knickers. Makes a change from stuffing his friggin' hands down 'em! Hi, I'm Rita.

(*Lights out.*)

Scene Two

Lights up. The five women stand in a row as at their entrance earlier in the play. GABBY *puts on some music.*

GABBY	Before we start, can we change into our boots.
FAITH	Oh I'd better go and get mine, I left 'em in the changing room.

(FAITH *exits.* TRISHA *is already wearing hers. The others take their boots from bags, start to pull them on.* SARAH *pulls out a pair of ankle boots. Everyone else has got knee-length boots.*)

SARAH	I wasn't sure what to bring. Will these do?

GABBY	Try and bring knee length in future. Sexier.
SARAH	Oh. Right.
BEV	(*as she pulls on boots*) So are you a professional pole dancer, Gabby?
GABBY	Used to be. I worked at a club in town.
RITA	Did you like it?
GABBY	The money was good. Shame about some of the clients.
RITA	Why did you give it up?
GABBY	I've a three year old son.
TRISHA	Aww, lovely. How long have you been married, Gabby? I've been married to Gareth for nearly a year. (*Glancing meaningfully at* BEV.) Isn't it lovely having a special man in your life?
GABBY	Wouldn't know. I'm a single parent. Are we more or less ready?
	(BEV *smirks at* TRISHA, *as* FAITH *enters – wearing huge hiking boots! She stops when she sees what the others are wearing. Looks down at her own.* TRISHA *and* RITA *start to kill themselves with laughter,* TRISHA *pointing at them.*)
RITA	(*laughing*) What you gonna do, Faith, *climb* the friggin' pole?!
	(*The others laugh, including* GABBY, *all except* BEV.)
BEV	Sorry, Faith, I should've told you.

RITA	Hey, Faith, d'you wanna lift after the class or are you just gonna hike it home?!
	(*She gives a big raucous laugh.*)
GABBY	Maybe you should do this session in bare feet.
	(*An embarrassed* FAITH *nods and takes off her boots.*)
GABBY	Can you take a pole one between two, please. (*Gestures to* SARAH.) You share with me. First thing your have to do is to learn to love your pole. So stroke it.
	(*She demonstrates.*)
RITA	(*as she strokes it*) Hello, gorgeous, d'you come here often?
BEV	(*simulates masturbating her pole*) Oh look, mine's getting bigger!
	(*They all laugh.*)
GABBY	Next thing I want you to do is to get your pelvis acquainted with the pole.
	(*She grinds her pelvis into the pole to demonstrate.*)
FAITH	I can't do that!
	(FAITH *and* SARAH *are very reticent but* BEV *grinds the pole like she's shagging it, making sexual noises.*)
GABBY	Don't get carried away, Bev. Next exercise. Hold onto the pole with both hands, lean back with your

	body at a 90 degree angle like you're sitting down on a couch . . . or a chair . . . or a man.
	(BEV *leans back.*)
BEV	I look like I'm having a crap!
	(*They all laugh. But* BEV *now struggles to get up.* GABBY *goes across to her.*)
	Are you okay?
BEV	Do I look okay?!
GABBY	D'you know the advantage of exercising like this?
BEV	You die healthier?
GABBY	(*smiles*) Your bodies will become so much more supple. But you're not going to find this easy, Bev.
BEV	Why not?
TRISHA	She's talking about your weight, Bev.
	(BEV *shoots her a look.*)
GABBY	Do you do much exercising, Bev?
BEV	I gave up jogging for me health when me thighs kept rubbing together and setting me tights on fire.
	(GABBY *finds this funny and laughs, as do the others. She takes* BEV'S *hand, pulls her up.*)
GABBY	What about dieting?
BEV	I'm on the garlic diet.

GABBY	Sorry, I don't know that.
BEV	You don't lose weight . . . but you look thinner from a distance.
	(*They all laugh.*)
GABBY	Moving on . . . we're now going to exercise your biceps. Pole dancing needs upper arm strength. Make sure your hands are dry and you have no cream on them, or you'll slip onto your bum. (*They do.*) Now I want you to take hold of the pole with both arms and try and lift yourself off the ground.
	(BEV *can't do it. She pretends to raise herself off the ground by just standing on her toes.*)
	Up. And down. Up again . . . and down . . . up again . . . and down. Carry on, keep doing it.
	(*They do.* SARAH *is also struggling badly.* RITA *and* TRISHA, *who are sharing a pole, jump up and down like pistons, faster and faster.*)
RITA	I feel sick!
BEV	This is easy.
GABBY	Bev, stop cheating. Lift your body off the ground. Come on.
	(*She tries, and raises her feet maybe a centimetre off the ground but then collapses onto her knees.*)
BEV	Faith, you have a go.
	(FAITH *tries – but she's hopeless.*)
GABBY	Well done. How many of you can do the splits?

(*Shock horror all round – except* TRISHA.)

RITA: Not since the kids.

TRISHA: (*hand up*) I can, Gabby.

GABBY: That's no problem. We'll try the jazz splits. You might surprise yourself.

BEV: Surprise? Be a bloody miracle.

GABBY: Stand behind me, watch and follow me, see how far you can stretch down. Okay . . . here we go. Don't force yourself or you'll pull a muscle.

(GABBY *slowly does the splits. The others are hopeless, getting so far, unable to move, stuck.* BEV *and* SARAH *fall over.* FAITH *seems stuck half way.*)

BEV: It's a long time since I opened me legs this wide.

GABBY: Well done all of you.

(FAITH *can't move.*)

FAITH: Er . . . excuse me. I'm stuck.

GABBY: Let's move on to your first pole exercise.

FAITH: No, I really am stuck.

(GABBY *sees her, goes to her. She holds her hand to pull her up, but to no effect. Eventually* FAITH *topples over and is able to stand.*)

GABBY: Are you okay?

FAITH: I've been better.

TRISHA	You'll have to lose weight, Bev.
BEV	Oh will I?
TRISHA	Quite frankly, Bev, with all that weight you'd be better suited to sumo wrestling than pole dancing.
	(*And regrets saying it as soon as she sees* BEV'S *face.* BEV *suddenly stands in a sumo wrestling position and charges at* TRISHA *with a frightening scream.* TRISHA *puts up her hands, totally scared.*)
	I'm sorry, I'm sorry, I'm sorry!
	(*And* BEV *stops within an inch of her, then relaxes, sees* TRISHA'S *utter fear, and smiles.*)
BEV	Good.
	(*Still smiling* BEV *turns and walks away, but suddenly swings back again and does a fierce cry.* TRISHA *jumps,* BEV *laughs again.*)
GABBY	You were out of order, Trisha.
TRISHA	Yes, I know – but I was only saying. Shall we continue?
	(GABBY *goes to the centre pole.*)
GABBY	(*a dig at* TRISHA) Thank you, Trisha. Okay, ladies, we're going to start off with a simple pole movement.
	(*She notices that* FAITH *is tugging at the back of her shorts, pulling a face.*)
GABBY	Are you all right?

FAITH	Yes, I've just got me knickers stuck up me bum. (*Pulls harder.*) Better. Sorry.
GABBY	Okay . . . if we're all ready. Any other problems?
	(TRISHA *puts up her hand.*)
	Yes?
TRISHA	Are there any exercises I can do to increase the size of my breasts?
GABBY	(*taken aback but patient*) Er, no.
TRISHA	Shame. Looks like I'll definitely have to have my boobs done.
GABBY	Now, ladies, watch this. It's called the Fireman move.
RITA	I once went out with a fireman.
BEV	Bet he was hot.
	(*They laugh.* GABBY *demonstrates.*)
GABBY	Walk round the pole, take hold of it with both hands, use your left leg for momentum, and swing. Easy, yes?
BEV	Really bloody easy!
	(GABBY *moves downstage away from the pole. The five of them move to a pole.*)
RITA	(*rubbing her hands up and down the pole*) This is the biggest pole I've ever had me hands round.

(BEV *laughs,* FAITH *stifles a laugh,* TRISHA *tuts, disgusted,* SARAH *seems slightly embarrassed.*)

BEV
You've been going out with the wrong fellahs.

GABBY
Okay, after three, one two three . . . and swing

(*They try the movement. They are all comically hopeless.*)

GABBY
Let's see some grace and elegance. Again, after three. One, two, three . . .

(BEV *tries it and she falls with a mighty crash.* GABBY *goes to her.*)

Are you all right?

(BEV *nods and gets up.*)

Maybe you now, Faith.

(FAITH *tries – one, two, three – hopeless.*)

Again.

(*This time she jumps up the pole with the aid of* BEV *pushing her up, then she slides very slowly down it, does a hand pirouette.*)

Swap over. Trisha . . .

TRISHA
Must I?

GABBY
Yes, please. Sarah . . .

(SARAH *steps up to the pole and* TRISHA *reluctantly steps off it.* TRISHA *watches* RITA *do the move again, then . . .*)

TRISHA	Gabby, can I have another go, Rita's taking an awfully long time.
GABBY	Seems a good idea to take a five minute break.
	(*She exits. All the women breathe out, relax, except* TRISHA *who looks pleased.*)
SARAH	I'm not sure about this.
RITA	So what you doing here, you must've known what it was going to be like?
SARAH	Yes, I know, I'm . . . I'm not sure what I am doing here.
FAITH	You're doing better than me and Bev.
SARAH	I don't know about that.
BEV	Stick with it.
FAITH	I didn't think I'd have to contort me body into all sorts of positions.
RITA	Yeh, I thought you just sort of shagged the pole . . .
TRISHA	Maybe, Rita, you're going about it the wrong way?
BEV	Listen to this, Rita, these words of advice could change your life.
TRISHA	No really. What I'm trying to say is . . . .my husband, Gareth . . . has never 'shagged' me.
	(*They all turn and look at her, 'what?'*)

	He makes **love** to me, he doesn't shag me. And maybe, Rita, instead of shagging the pole, if you made love to it . . . in a sensuous way of course . . .
RITA	. . . Then the pole might have an orgasm? Fuck off whatever your fucking name is!
TRISHA	(*pompous*) It's Trisha . . . and please don't talk to me like that, I was only saying.
BEV	(*to* TRISHA) This husband o' yours, Gareth . . . sounds a bit too bloody perfect.
TRISHA	He is perfect. Everything about him. I still can't believe how lucky I was to find him.
RITA	So you been married nearly a year?
TRISHA	(*proud*) Ten months two weeks and six days.
RITA	Can't you be more precise?
TRISHA	Well we got married at 2.00 o'clock so it's exactly ten months, two weeks, six days and . . . (*Glancing at watch.*) . . . five hours.
RITA	. . . And sixteen minutes.
TRISHA	Precisely.
RITA	D'you have any kids?
TRISHA	Oh no, not yet. But I do have a little Shitsu.
RITA	I'm not surprised.
BEV	D'you know the difference between a new husband and a new dog? (TRISHA *shakes head.*) After a year the dog's still excited to see you.

(RITA *laughs.*)

TRISHA	Oh yes, very funny. Well Gareth and I intend to keep our relationship fresh and exciting.
RITA	How? You gonna have affairs?
TRISHA	You've either never met the right man or you're divorced.
RITA	Take it from me, love, there's no such thing as the perfect man or the perfect relationship.
FAITH	Personally, I'm not bothered about meeting the perfect man – (*Beat.*) – any man'd do for me.
TRISHA	Desperation is not attractive in a woman, Faith.
BEV	Trisha!
TRISHA	I'm only saying! If she sets her sights low . . .
BEV	She'll only meet short men?

(RITA *and* FAITH *laugh.*)

TRISHA	You married, Sarah?

(*She seems reluctant to open up.*)

SARAH	Yes.
TRISHA	How long?
SARAH	(*beat*) Twenty six years.
TRISHA	Oh fantastic.
RITA	And is he perfect?

SARAH	Who is?
RITA	Exactly!
TRISHA	And do you have any children?
SARAH	Yes. Two.
TRISHA	How old?
SARAH	Nineteen and twenty one.
RITA	(*to* TRISHA) And does your husband know you're here?

(SARAH *looks down.*)

Hey, no sweat. Neither does mine. He thinks I've gone maypole dancing!

(*Lights down.*)

Scene Three

Lights up. They are individually working on the pole. Currently it's TRISHA *and she looks quite confident. She finishes.* GABBY *turns the music down with a remote control.*

GABBY	Very good, Trisha, you're spinning well. Loved your back-bend. But well done, you've set the standard.
TRISHA	(*chuffed*) Thank you. And how were my breasts?
GABBY	Sorry?
TRISHA	Did they look firm . . . you know, as I performed?

GABBY	I don't know, Trisha, I wasn't looking at your breasts.
TRISHA	No, no, of course you weren't – but don't you think this top makes them look smaller?
BEV	Will you shut up about your frigging breasts, you're getting on my tits.
GABBY	Can we move on, Trisha. Okay, Faith, your turn.

(*She looks like 'do I have to?'*)

You're amongst friends, you'll be fine.

(BEV *winks at her, nods 'go on'. Nervously she approaches the pole.*)

Just remember what I've taught you over the last four weeks. Take your time.

(GABBY *turns the music up. Nervously,* FAITH *tries the movements on the pole. She is totally hopeless.* TRISHA *starts laughing and* BEV *digs her hard in her ribs and* TRISHA *doubles up.* FAITH *collapses from the pole in a heap.* GABBY *stops the music.*)

Good try, anyway, Faith. Rita.

(RITA *walks towards the pole, sexy, full of confidence.* TRISHA *is sitting on her podium.*)

RITA	Hey, hop it, face ache.

(*The music starts.*)

GABBY	And keep those toes pointed, Rita.

(RITA *attempts various spins on the pole but it looks awkward. She tries again. Better. Then she turns to the others, smiles and walks back pleased. They clap.*)

Sarah . . .

(SARAH *is nervous, looks reluctant.*)

BEV Go on, chuck, you can do it!

(*And* SARAH *throws back her shoulders, approaches the pole with confidence – but as soon as the music starts, the confidence dissipates. She turns to* GABBY.)

SARAH I'm sorry, this just isn't me. I don't feel right, I've made a big mistake.

(*She starts to walk off.*)

BEV (*after her*) Sarah! Watch. Put on my favourite, Gabby.

(BEV *nods to* GABBY *who switches on the music and it's a raunchy number.* BEV *rises to the occasion by sexily moving towards the pole – but instead of performing on the pole, she does her own 'thing', using the pole as if it's a fellow dancer, rubbing against it, mock sexiness, hilarious, shoving her bum up and down, then waggling her bum at the others.* SARAH *has returned, amused.*)

GABBY That is not a pole dance, Bev.

BEV Really?

(*Lights out.*)

Scene Four

Open on the village hall. GABBY *is ready as* BEV, FAITH, RITA *and* SARAH *enter.*

GABBY   Are we all okay?

              (*They all say 'yeh'.*)

              Feeling fit?

BEV   No.

GABBY   Where's Trisha?

TRISHA   (*entering*) Here I am. (*All breezy.*) And I've got some great news. I've been given a date for my cosmetic surgery, isn't that fantastic?

BEV   (*sarcastic*) Fantastic.

GABBY   Are you sure about this, Trisha?

TRISHA   Absolutely.

FAITH   But you've already got very nice breasts – both of them.

TRISHA   And I'm going to have even nicer breasts, bigger, firmer, more uplift . . .

SARAH   Trisha, is this the most important thing in your life, having enlarged breasts?

TRISHA   Apart from Gareth? Of course it is!

SARAH   Then you're a very shallow, young woman.

TRISHA	Sarah, there's no need to be jealous, you could have plastic surgery yourself if you wanted.
SARAH	I beg your pardon?
TRISHA	No woman need have sagging breasts.
SARAH	You silly girl! You silly, stupid girl!
TRISHA	(*taken by surprise*) What?
SARAH	I am going to have plastic surgery!
TRISHA	Sorry?
SARAH	You want bigger breasts!? Here! Have this one!
	(*And from her top she pulls out a prosthetic breast, throws it at* TRISHA. *Everyone is utterly stunned. Long silence. Eventually.*)
SARAH	I've had a mastectomy.
FAITH	(*to* BEV) But I thought you could only have a vasectomy if you're a man.
BEV	She's lost a breast.
FAITH	(*suddenly realising and feeling stupid*) Oh, oh of course! Sorry! I feel so stupid! Sorry, Sarah, oh that's awful.
RITA	When did you have the op?
SARAH	Six months ago.
FAITH	Oh you poor thing.
	(TRISHA *feels awful.*)

TRISHA	Sarah, I'm ... I am so so sorry. I am a stupid, silly girl, wittering on about myself when all the time, all the time you were ...
RITA	You've had your chemo and they caught it in time?
	(SARAH *nods. Pause as they still take this in.*)
GABBY	So why did you join my class?
BEV	Yeh, I mean ... pole dancing?!
RITA	Yeh, why pole dancing?!
SARAH	(*reluctantly*) Well ... since ... since the operation, I've felt, I suppose I've felt ... well ashamed of my body, my scars ... I've lost confidence in myself. ... as a woman ... and er Roger ... my husband ... I haven't let him near me ... I've lost my libido.
FAITH	You know, Sarah, I'm always losing my mobile so you should do what I do, think about where you last had it then retrace your steps.
BEV	Faith, libido is your sexual desire.
FAITH	Is it? Oh yeh! Course it is! Sorry. Sorry, Sarah.
SARAH	So anyway, I thought by coming here, it might give me back some confidence in myself and my body.
BEV	Christ, that is one bloody brave thing to do ... putting yourself through this ...
SARAH	... But I think maybe I've made a big mistake.
	(*And suddenly they're all round her persuading her otherwise: "No", "No, you've not", "You're great", "You can't give up", "No way are you*

giving up", "No way", "That's right", "We're all in this together", "Yeh!".)

GABBY   They're right. They're right, Sarah. You're not giving up, we're all in this together.

(*Lights out.*)

Scene Five

RITA *has arrived first. She is on her mobile.*

RITA   I'll be back in a couple of hours, darling, so get yourself ready, the table's booked for eight. Love you loads.

(*Switches off mobile as* GABBY *enters.*)

GABBY   You're early.

RITA   I'm keen. (*Then.*) Did you earn good money when you were pole-dancing?

GABBY   Yes, very good. Why?

RITA   That club you worked in . . . they're advertising for older women to do pole dancing.

GABBY   So I believe. There's quite a niche apparently.

RITA   Wouldn't mind giving it a try. Gabby, what d'you reckon me chances are . . . you know, of getting a job in your old club?

(GABBY *eyes up* RITA.)

GABBY   You've a great figure.

RITA	Ta.
GABBY	And you're very sexy.
RITA	Don't fancy me, do you? (GABBY *laughs.*) So d'you reckon I could be good enough?
GABBY	Let's see how you progress, it's early days but you're doing fine.

(*As they start to get ready, we hear off the voices of* FAITH, BEV *and* SARAH.)

FAITH	(*off*) I can't pole dance in these!
BEV	(*off*) Course you can.
SARAH	(*off*) Take them off for the pole dancing.

(*And they enter.* FAITH *totters on unsteadily in high heeled boots – but she's also been made up – new hair do completely different – new set of clothes – and she's hardly recognisable.* RITA *and* GABBY *are gob-smacked when they see her.*)

RITA	Faith!!
SARAH	What d'you think?
GABBY	I'm gob-smacked.

(*As* TRISHA *enters.*)

BEV	It took us three hours to get her like this mind. Take your coat off, Faith.

(FAITH *takes off her coat and underneath she is wearing a stunning black dress.* RITA *and* TRISHA *are wowed.*)

Trisha	Oh wow, Faith, you look fantastic.
Bev	Coming from you that's a real compliment.
Sarah	We took her shopping.
Trisha	Not where she normally goes then – Oxfam.
Bev	That's more like it.
Trisha	Only joking.
Bev	I'm taking her clubbing later. (*To* Rita.) . . . fancy coming?
Rita	Bloody love to . . . but can't . . . it's my daughter's birthday.
Bev	How old is she?
Rita	Er, fifteen.
Bev	You're bloody joking!
Rita	I'll come with you next time you go.
Bev	Gabby, you fancy it?
Gabby	Sorry, got to get back for my son.
Trisha	I'll come.
Bev	(*unenthusiastic*) Really? You sure?
Trisha	I'd like to come.
Bev	It might not be your thing.
Trisha	I like dancing.

Bev	Won't your Gareth be expecting you home?
Trisha	He will . . . but he's very understanding. I'll check it out with him first. Won't be a sec.
Bev	(*mouths*) Fucking hell!
	(*She takes out her mobile, moves upstage. The others gather round* Faith.)
Faith	(*to* Rita) So you think lads'll fancy me?
Rita	If they don't, they want their heads feeling.
Faith	It's not their heads I want to feel. Ooooo. (*She laughs as do the others.*) I can't believe I've said that.
Gabby	Okay, let's get started. You know, Faith, you can't pole dance in that lovely dress.
Bev	Show her, Faith.
	(*And* Faith *unzips her dress, drops it, and underneath she's wearing a brand new, trendy, classy hot pants and t-shirt. She spins round proudly. Another 'wow' factor – as* Trisha *returns from making her phone call.*)
Trisha	Anyway, it's not a problem with Gareth. In fact he said if we give him a ring when we're ready to come home from the club, he'll come and pick us all up.
Faith	Oh that's very nice of him, Trisha.
Trisha	He's a very nice man, Faith.
Bev	Has he got a big one?

TRISHA	I beg your pardon?!
BEV	His car!
TRISHA	No, it's a . . . it's a Skoda.
BEV	A Skoda!
TRISHA	A Skoda . . . estate.
BEV	That'll be bloody brilliant if we all cop off!!
TRISHA	I will not be copping off with anyone, thank you very much.
BEV	I bloody will. Watch out, fellahs, Bev's had a wash!
	(*Lights out.*)

Scene Six

Lights up. Village hall. BEV, FAITH *followed by* SARAH *and* RITA *arrive for the class.*

RITA	So go on, spill the bloody beans.
FAITH	What d'you mean?
SARAH	What was he like? Gareth. When he gave you the lift home.
RITA	He was a wanker, wasn't he?
FAITH	No, he was lovely.
RITA	Lovely?

FAITH	Yeh.
RITA	Lovely! Bev?
BEV	Yeh. Sorry to disappoint you but he was a really nice guy.
SARAH	You're not . . . well, winding us up?
FAITH	And he was good-looking.
BEV	And charming . . .
RITA	Fuck me!
BEV	. . . In fact he was everything she'd described.
SARAH	So what's he doing with Trisha . . . sorry, that's bitchy.
RITA	No, you're right, what is he doing with Trisha?
BEV	Anyone's guess. Who can get inside the brain of a man?
RITA	No one. It's not big enough.

(*They laugh.*)

SARAH	And how did you get on at the club, Faith?
FAITH	Oh I had a great time. We danced, didn't we, Bev?
BEV	Yeh, we danced.
FAITH	And we had a few drinks.
BEV	Quite a few drinks. The guys were eyeing her up.

FAITH	No, they weren't! She's lying.
BEV	They were. Though they never did anything about it.
FAITH	Actually one came to speak to me.
BEV	When? I never saw that!
FAITH	You and Trisha were in the loo.
BEV	Why didn't you say something?
FAITH	Well it was nothing really.
SARAH	What did he say?
FAITH	Oh he just came up to me and said, "How do you like your eggs in the morning?"
	(*The other three all chime "NO!"*)
	Yeh.
SARAH	He didn't!
FAITH	He did.
BEV	I hope you said unfertilised.
FAITH	(*not getting it*) Sorry?
SARAH	So what did you say?
FAITH	Well I thought it was a very odd question to ask but I told him I don't actually eat eggs for my breakfast, I prefer a bowl of cereal, usually Special K with semi-skimmed milk, no sugar, followed by a round of toast with low-fat margarine.

(*They all nod as she says this. They're thrown for a second, as they share a look.*)

RITA
And what did he say after that?

FAITH
Well actually he said nothing. He had this sort of glazed look and he just turned round and walked away, didn't say a word.

(*They are thrown again as they share looks.*)

BEV
Faith, it was a chat-up line.

FAITH
What was?

BEV
How do you like your eggs in the morning. It's a corny chat-up line.

FAITH
No!

SARAH
He was asking to stay the night, Faith.

FAITH
No?!!

(*They all nod 'yes'.*)

I've been chatted up?

(*They all nod.*)

I have been chatted up! I was chatted up at the club! *I was chatted up at the club!!* And he wanted to cook me breakfast!

BEV
No. He wanted to shag you.

FAITH
No! Did he?! He wanted to shag me! Someone wanted to shag me!

SARAH	But what was he like, Faith?
	(*And this tops her in her tracks. She thinks.*)
FAITH	Well . . . actually . . . he was . . . he was ugly, he was *really* ugly.
SARAH	Then maybe it was a lucky escape, Faith. Hey, don't you dare sell yourself cheaply. (*She puts a motherly arm round her.*) You're too special and you're too nice.
FAITH	Am I?
	(SARAH *nods.*)
	Aww, thank you, Sarah. You're lovely, you are.
BEV	He couldn't have been as ugly as the guy who tried to chat me up.
FAITH	I thought he was rather nice.
BEV	Faith, he was so ugly if he put his head out the window he'd be arrested for mooning!
	(*They all laugh.*)
	He came up to me and said, haven't I seen you some place before?
RITA	And you said, yeh, that's why I don't go there any more!
	(*They laugh.*)
BEV	And then he said what d'you do for a living and I said . . . I'm a drag queen.

RITA	I'll remember that line.
BEV	No, but his mouth dropped open and he said, "You're not, are you?"
SARAH	No!
BEV	... Which made me feel great. I mean, do I look like a drag queen?
RITA	Well actually ...
BEV	Don't answer that you.

(*As* GABBY *enters, they all say "Hi", then* TRISHA *enters. They all say "Hi" to her but she doesn't reply, she's reticent, withdrawn.*)

SARAH	You okay, Trish? (*Shakes head.*) What's wrong?
TRISHA	Gareth and me ... we've just had our first big argument ...
SARAH	Oh I'm sorry.
TRISHA	(*upset*) ... And it was horrible ...
SARAH	What was it about?
TRISHA	I was telling Gareth about you, Sarah ... hope you don't mind ...
SARAH	Course not ...
TRISHA	... About your breast cancer and how bad I felt and he asked why and I confessed to him how I'd been planning to have my breasts enlarged and he just went like crazy. He said, "What?", you know really shouted, and he kept saying, "Why? Why? Why?",

and I said I was doing it for him and that seemed to make him worse and he started ranting at me, saying he didn't want me to do things for him and that I was driving him mad and I shouldn't change for him I should do it for myself and he's always liked me as I am.

(*She starts crying.*)

SARAH Trisha. Gareth's right.

RITA Yeh, he is. Do it for yourself.

GABBY And if he's always liked you as you are, that's great.

SARAH That's fantastic, Trish, look on it as a positive thing.

GABBY Anyway, why do you want to change yourself, Trisha?

TRISHA 'Cos I have to.

SARAH Why?

TRISHA 'Cos I have to get away from that fat, ugly girl I was. And sometimes I look in the mirror and I still see that girl and it frightens me and I can't believe Gareth ever fell for me and I just feel lucky and I have to please him. And I'm scared one day I'll wake up and I'll be back at school again and I'll be fat and everyone 'll be laughing at me.

BEV Trish, they didn't laugh at you 'cos you were fat . . .

TRISHA They did . . .

BEV I was fatter than you, they didn't laugh at me.

TRISHA	'Cos you were tough and mouthy and you made everyone laugh.
BEV	Exactly. D'you think I was born that way? I wasn't. I made meself be like that 'cos it was the only way to survive.
FAITH	Trisha, you're gorgeous.
TRISHA	I'm not.
	(*And they all reassure her that she is. "You are", "Course you are", "You're beautiful".*)
FAITH	And when I met you I thought . . . I wish I could be as confident as her.
TRISHA	So why do I still feel ugly?
	(*And she looks so vulnerable.*)
GABBY	Okay, Trisha, that's it, you're in my class, you do as I say right? (*No reaction.*) Right? (TRISHA *nods.*) Say after me, I am not ugly, I am absolutely gorgeous.
	(*Which makes* TRISHA *smile.*)
	Go on, say it.
TRISHA	I can't say that.
GABBY	You can. Go on – say it. (*A moment.*) I am not ugly . . . go on.
TRISHA	I am not ugly . . .
GABBY	I am totally, irresistibly gorgeous.

TRISHA (*laughing*) I'm not saying that!

BEV Yes, you frigging are . . . go on, say it.

TRISHA I am totally . . . (*Pauses. They nod for her to carry on.*) I am totally, irresistibly gorgeous.

(*She laughs, they all laugh. Then.*)

TRISHA You know you're the best friends I've ever had. (*Beat.*) Would you all like to come to my wedding anniversary party?

(*Which takes them all by surprise. Behind her* BEV *is shaking her head.*)

It's in a couple of weeks' time. Gareth's ordered a marquee for our garden.

SARAH That's very nice of you, Trisha.

TRISHA I'd like you all to come.

(*Silence.*)

RITA So who's going to be there?

TRISHA Well my parents and Gareth's parents and his brother and sister-in-law . . . (*Pause.*)

RITA And . . . ?

TRISHA Well it's just a small affair.

(*Beat, as they take in that* TRISHA *has no friends.*)

SARAH I'd love to come, Trisha.

TRISHA Oh thank you. And you will bring Roger?

SARAH	Yes, I'm sure he'd love to come.
TRISHA	And Gabby, Bev and Faith . . . and Rita I suppose . . . so long as you don't swear in front of our parents?
RITA	As if I fucking would! (*On* TRISHA's *face.*) Joke.
TRISHA	And you're married, aren't you, Rita, would you like to bring your husband?
RITA	You're friggin' joking! We never go out together! Apart from family weddings and funerals.
BEV	How long you been married?
RITA	Too long.
BEV	So why don't you leave him?
RITA	(*ignoring this*) Can I bring my two girls?
TRISHA	Course you can.
FAITH	And we'd love to come, wouldn't we, Bev?
	(BEV *is shaking her head behind* TRISHA's *back.*)
TRISHA	Oh brilliant! It'll be lovely to have all my friends around me on our special day. Now I think we should practice our pole dancing moves, don't you?
GABBY	If you say so, Trisha.
TRISHA	. . . Particularly you, Bev.
	(*And* BEV *gives* TRISHA *a V-sign behind her back.*)

FAITH	Hey, Rita, we've decided we're going to that club again tonight, fancy coming?
RITA	Love to. I'll have to check with the girls that their lazy sod of a Dad can look after 'em. (*Turning to* SARAH.) Fancy coming along?
SARAH	I really don't think it's my thing.
FAITH	Aww, come on, Sarah, it'll be a laugh.
SARAH	I'm too old for clubs.
RITA	Don't be a boring old fart. Ring Roger and tell him you're on a girls' night out.

(*Beat.* FAITH *looks at her imploringly, "Please".*)

SARAH	Okay, I'll come.

(*As they all say, "Yes".*)

FAITH	Oh and Sarah, if a guy comes up to you and asks what you eat for breakfast – pass him on to me!

(*As they laugh, lights fade.*)

Scene Seven

Lights up. The village hall. BEV, FAITH, TRISHA *and* RITA *enter, they're laughing, giggling.* GABBY *is already there.*

BEV	(*mouthing to* GABBY) Faith got off with a guy last week at the club.
GABBY	Hey! Fantastic!

FAITH	Hey, Gabby, I copped off last Wednesday!
GABBY	(*mock innocence*) No! What was he like?
FAITH	Lovely. Hey, and the coincidence is . . . it turns out he's just started work in the men's wear department at our place . . .
BEV	. . . Though he's really into women's lingerie.
FAITH	Bev! His name's Richard but he prefers Richie 'cos his full name is Richard Frick and he hated it 'cos at school they called him Dick Prick.
	(*They all laugh.*)
	You'd better not laugh when you meet him!
RITA	Oh we're gonna meet him, are we?
BEV	She's been out with him twice this week!
TRISHA	Twice! Already?
FAITH	He took me out for a meal three nights ago.
GABBY	Where to?
FAITH	Burger King.
RITA	Burger King!?
BEV	He's big on romance.
FAITH	I like Burger King!
RITA	Did he have a Big Whopper?

FAITH   No, he had . . . (*And as the others laughs, she gets it.*) Oh! You!

TRISHA   I know what I would've said to my Gareth if he'd taken me to Burger King on our first date.

FAITH   And then last night he took me to the dogs.

RITA   Hey, you wanna get a ring on him quick, he sounds a great catch!

FAITH   We had a very nice time, thank you very much, he won twenty pounds and afterwards we celebrated and he bought me fish and chips and mushy peas and we ate in the park on a bench.

RITA   Bloody hell, he sounds like my fellah. The only time we have a candle-lit dinner is when there's a power cut.

           (*They laugh.*)

           You know he's found out I'm coming here.

BEV   How?

RITA   The bugger followed me here last week.

BEV   You're joking!

RITA   So I told him straight, I wanted to be a proper pole dancer.

TRISHA   What did he say to that?

RITA   Well when he picked himself up off the floor, he said, "At your age, you must be bloody joking!" So I told him about this club in town advertising for women over 35 and he said, "I'm not having dirty

	old blokes ogling my naked wife as she rubs herself up against some frigging pole!" So I said, "I've tried rubbing meself up against you, you're not interested 'less you're pissed."
FAITH	You didn't!
RITA	And he said, "When was the last time you came onto me?", so I told him straight . . .
GABBY	What?
RITA	"I could wriggle me tits in your face and you'd accuse me of causing a draught!"
FAITH	No!
	(*And they all laugh.*)
RITA	And then he got all tough . . . "Well you're doing this over my dead body!" – So I've arranged the Co-op to do the funeral next week.
	(*They all laugh.*)
	Anyway, enough of me . . . come on, Faith, this fellah of yours . . . have you shagged him yet?
FAITH	Rita! Of course I've not! I've only known him a week!
RITA	You must at least've snogged him.
FAITH	Well yes, we have kissed.
TRISHA	Tongues?
FAITH	Of course!

RITA	Have you touched his willy yet?
GABBY	What are you girls like?!
RITA	Well have you?
FAITH	No! We're taking it slowly.
BEV	An inch at a time.
FAITH	Bev! (*Pauses, then smiles as she remembers.*) But you know . . . we did almost get carried away last night . . . on the bench after we'd finished our fish and chips . . .
TRISHA	How?
FAITH	I let him touch me . . . you know, up here. (*Her breasts.*) And then he tried to undo me bra – and I was going to let him – but then his fingers kept slipping 'cos of all the grease on 'em from the fish and chips.
	(*They all laugh.*)
	What's so funny?
RITA	And when you seeing him again?
FAITH	Tonight.
TRISHA	He must be very keen then. (FAITH *smiles, 'he must'.*) Are you his first girl friend?
FAITH	No! His second.
TRISHA	You sound perfect.
RITA	And d'you like him?

TRISHA	Of course she likes him, beggers can't be choosers.
GABBY	Trisha!
FAITH	As a matter of fact, Trisha, if I'd had to choose from all the fellahs at that club, I would've chosen him.
RITA	That told you, big gob! You haven't bloody changed, have you?
TRISHA	I was only –
	(*And they all chorus "SAYING"* – TRISHA *laughs.*)
GABBY	I wonder where Sarah is? Well we can't wait for her. Okay, two on each pole. This will be great for your flexibility. (*Demonstrates.*) Stroke, stroke, turn, leg nearest pole, and slid down, leg up, and I want your partner to stretch, push and push, then smack. Take turns.
TRISHA	Me first.
BEV	(*to* FAITH) Watch her.
	(TRISHA *does the movement,* RITA *pushes her leg back really far and* TRISHA *cries out but not as much as when* RITA *smacks* TRISHA *really hard. Now* RITA *and* TRISHA *exchange and* BEV *works with* FAITH, *but* FAITH *pushes* BEV's *leg too far and she cries out.*)
GABBY	Yes, very elegant. You do need to lose more weight, Bev. Have you thought about swimming? Swimming's very good for your figure.
BEV	So how come whales are so fat?

GABBY	(*she laughs, then*) Let's swap over. And after you've done that I want you to show me tonight how much you've learnt and how far you've come.
	(*And in the middle of it, a stoney-faced* SARAH *enters. She stops, watches them.* GABBY *sees her watching and stops the music.*)
	Just in time to show us how much you've learned, Sarah.
	(RITA *immediately picks up what is wrong.*)
RITA	You okay, Sarah?
	(SARAH *shakes her head, her face crumbles and she starts to cry.*)
SARAH	I've found a lump . . . in my other breast.
	(*Lights out.*)

Scene Eight

Lights up. The village hall. Music. GABBY, FAITH, TRISHA *and* RITA *are sitting on the floor having a cup of tea.* BEV *enters from door.*

BEV	Still no sign of Sarah.
FAITH	Are we going to wait for her?
GABBY	Can't wait much longer, we're ten minutes late starting already.
RITA	It's got to be bad news or she'd be here.
BEV	She'll come, bad news or good news.

TRISHA	Oh God, I hope she's all right.
FAITH	Oh so do I, I think it's awful.
	(*As they ponder this,* GABBY *breaks it up.*)
GABBY	D'you think we should do some stretches?
	(*They all agree, stand – as* SARAH *enters.* SARAH's *looking dejected.*)
TRISHA	(*seeing her*) Sarah . . .
	(*They all turn to her.*)
RITA	You got the results of your the CT scan?
	(SARAH *nods.*)
	And?
SARAH	(*small smile*) Not good.
RITA	Has it spread?
	(SARAH *nods.*)
	How far?
	(SARAH *shrugs, 'far enough'.*)
	So is it . . . is it . . . ?
SARAH	Terminal? Yes.
	(*Stunned silence – then* FAITH *pipes up.*)
FAITH	Oh well that's not too bad then.

(*They stare at* Faith, *can't believe what she's said. Eventually.*)

Sarah: Faith, terminal means I'm going to die.

(*A moment while* Faith *takes this in.*)

Faith: No! No! I thought it meant you just had it for a short term. Oh Sarah, I'm sorry, I'm sorry, I'm sorry . . .

(*And she bursts into tears, she's almost hysterical.* Sarah *goes to her, puts her arms round her, comforts her.*)

Sarah: Hey, come on, Faith, don't get upset. I'm going to be all right – well I'm not but if you get upset you'll only upset me more.

Trisha: Yes, pull yourself together, you're not the one who's dying!

(*And* Bev, Gabby *and* Rita *shoot her a look.*)

Sorry. Bit tactless?

Sarah: Just a bit, Trisha.

Faith: Maybe they got it wrong, maybe you're going to be all right . . .

Sarah: No, Faith . . . I'm not going to be all right, but I'm not going to give in to it either. I'll do everything I can to beat it. I've done it once, I'll do it again.

Rita: That's it, Sarah, you gotta be positive.

Gabby: Rita's right . . .

BEV	Yeh, she is . . .
FAITH	So maybe you're going to be okay, maybe you'll get better.
SARAH	(*sceptical*) Maybe . . .
GABBY	How was Roger when you told him?
	(*A moment.*)
SARAH	Upset. Obviously. But then we talked. We've hardly talked these last six months. I mean really talked. I'd shut him out. And we drank . . . and we cried . . . and we drank some more . . . and we laughed and we cuddled . . . and for the first time since my mastectomy . . . I think we made love.
BEV	Think?!
SARAH	It's a bit hazy. We were so . . .
RITA	Pissed?
SARAH	Totally totally pissed. And it was great. Well it wasn't. But it made us feel better. But I can't remember half of what we said or did – so I won't be doing it again . . . because I want to remember every single moment of what's left of my life.
FAITH	Oh Sarah.
SARAH	There's no point in wallowing in self pity . . . so I'm going to use it as an opportunity . . . to do all the things I've wanted to do . . .
TRISHA	Such as?

SARAH	Well for what's left of my life . . . six months, twelve months, twelve years . . . I want to be dangerous and surprise people and do things I've never done before.
BEV	Like what?
SARAH	Ohhh . . . parachuting . . . bungee jumping . . . sex with another woman . . .
	(*They all go "Nooooo!"*)
	That last one was a joke.
FAITH	Oh Sarah, how can you laugh . . . you're so brave.
SARAH	Oh no I'm not. I'm scared. If I'm honest I'm scared . . . well . . . well . . .
RITA	Shitless?
SARAH	Precisely. I'm scared shitless. I don't want to die. I'm not ready to die! But what I'm scared of . . . is getting so ill, I can't do anything and I have to rely on Roger, I don't want that.
RITA	Have you told the kids?
SARAH	(*shakes head*) Not yet.
FAITH	Oh Sarah.
SARAH	But I want to give something back before I go.
GABBY	How?
SARAH	Well . . . I hope you're going to help . . . all of you.
FAITH	Of course we will . . . any way we can.

SARAH	You might not say that when I explain what I want you to do.
RITA	Go on.
SARAH	We put on a charity pole dance show . . . for Cancer Research . . . the six of us . . . here . . . if that's okay with you, Gabby?
GABBY	Of course it is.

(*Pause as they take this in.*)

FAITH	A charity pole dance?

(SARAH *nods.*)

Us pole dancing?

(SARAH *nods.*)

In front of . . . men?

SARAH	. . . And women . . .
FAITH	. . . and they'd be watching us . . . as we . . . ?
BEV	. . . Make friggin' fools of ourselves.
SARAH	Probably.

(*Pause.*)

FAITH	Oh dear.
BEV	Oh shit.
RITA	Oh fuck.

(*Lights down. End of Act One.*)

ACT TWO

Scene One

Lights up. Village hall. Music.

The five women are finishing off a not very proficient pole dance movement and a dance routine. FAITH *and* BEV *in particular are still comically bad,* SARAH *struggles.* GABBY *switches down the music.*

GABBY	Well done, girls, that was totally, totally . . . pathetic. If you don't want people laughing at you, you're going to have to work harder. Okay, five minutes.
	(*She exits, then stops.*)
	By the way, Trisha, thank you for your anniversary party, really enjoyed it.
TRISHA	No, thank you for coming. And it was lovely to meet your little one, he's ever so sweet.
GABBY	Thank you.
	(*She exits.*)
TRISHA	Did anyone find out who the father is?
	(*They all say 'no'.*)
TRISHA	Oh and Rita, I thought your two girls were absolutely charming and so polite.
RITA	Thanks.
TRISHA	In fact I couldn't believe you're their mother.
BEV	Nice one, big gob.

Trisha	Sorry, that sounded awful, didn't it?
	(Rita *doesn't answer. During this scene she seems withdrawn, something on her mind.*)
Faith	You've got a lovely house, Trisha.
Bev	Yeh, how can you afford a place like that?
Trisha	Gareth's father's very rich, he paid for it.
Bev	What does he do?
Trisha	He owns a chain of pawn shops.
	(*Thinking she means 'porn' they all say Nooooo!*)
	Yeh.
Bev	Bloody hell! So that's where you get all your sexy gear from?
Trisha	Er . . . sorry? (*Then realising.*) Oh noooo! It's pawn as in p-a-w-n.
	(*And they all laugh.*)
	But anyway, thank you all for coming. Gareth enjoyed meeting you all.
Sarah	He's a very nice guy.
Trisha	Well he certainly liked you. He spent more time talking to you lot than he did to me! I hardly saw him.
Sarah	Everything all right between you now?
Trisha	(*covering*) Oh yes, absolutely perfect.

(She forces a smile. SARAH sneaks a glance at the others.)

Anyway, I think we should practice our pole routines, don't you?

(She goes to a pole, starts practising. The others don't follow.)

BEV   Teacher's pet. *(Changing tack.)* I once went out with a pole.

FAITH   I didn't know you'd been to Poland.

BEV   I mean he was long and thin.

FAITH   Greg?

BEV   That's him. Skinny as a chopstick. We looked the perfect couple.

TRISHA   *(stopping her routine)* I could never go out with a man who didn't have a firm, muscled, well toned body like my Gareth. What did you see in him?

BEV   He had a huge cock.

FAITH   Bev!

BEV   He did. In fact his cock was thicker than his waist.

FAITH   I'm sorry, Sarah. She has sex on the brain you know.

BEV   Well I've tried every other position. *(Laughs then.)* Anyway, I nearly killed poor Greg you know.

SARAH   How?

BEV	We'd just had sex, I was on top . . .
TRISHA	Too much information, Bev.
BEV	. . . And I'd just come . . .
TRISHA	Far too much information.
BEV	. . . And I collapsed on top of him . . .
TRISHA	The mind boggles.
BEV	And I lay for a few minutes . . . you know, sated, when I realised Greg wasn't moving, was hardly breathing. (*Pauses.*) He had his nose stuck between me tits and he was suffocating.

(*They laugh.*)

BEV	His face was blue. I had to give him mouth to mouth. And boy, he bloody loved that.
FAITH	Wonder what they'd have put on his death certificate as cause of death?

(*They laugh.*)

SARAH	On his headstone they could've put, "He'd only just come, then he was gone".
FAITH	(*laughing, surprised*) Sarah!

(*And* SARAH *is very amused at her own joke.* GABBY *has entered.* SARAH *sees that* RITA *has been a bit distant.*)

SARAH	You okay, Rita?
RITA	Yeh, why?

SARAH	Bit quiet – for you. (RITA *doesn't respond.*) What is it?
	(*A moment.*)
	Something bothering you?
RITA	I left my husband two nights ago.
	(*And they all go, "What?"*)
	It's all her fault you know.
SARAH	Me? Why?
RITA	You gave me the inspiration to do it.
SARAH	I did?
RITA	Watching you . . . what you're doing . . . made me realise . . . staying with Terry . . . it's wasting my life. And life's too short to waste it. So two nights ago me and the girls moved in with me Mam . . . until I sort something better.
SARAH	Good God. How did he react?
RITA	Not great.
BEV	What the hell did he say?
RITA	He jumped off that sofa like City had just scored. You're leaving ME?! Then he accused me of having another fellah . . .
TRISHA	As if . . .
RITA	He started throwing the furniture around, screaming . . . it was scary and the girls were terrified . . .

FAITH	Oh Rita, it sounds awful . . .
RITA	. . . But God, I felt so relieved when I got out that door. So thanks, Sarah.
SARAH	Oh God, Rita, I hope you've done the right thing.
RITA	I have. I know I have.
SARAH	It's a huge step for you though, Rita.
RITA	I know.
BEV	What did you say to the girls?
RITA	I just told 'em the truth – I said, your dad's become a boring, selfish, ignorant wanker and me and him haven't had a decent shag in six years!
FAITH	You didn't?!
	(RITA *gives her a look which says, "Course not".*)
RITA	I should've done it years ago. Soon as it started going bad . . . but,. you know . . . it's not easy . . .
	(*She looks upset.*)
SARAH	(*picking up on this*) What is it? (*A moment.*) Rita?
RITA	They're frightened of him you know. The girls.
SARAH	Frightened of their own dad? (RITA *nods.*) Why?
RITA	He's one of these guys who doesn't say much but when he goes . . . God, the temper on him.
FAITH	Really?

RITA	I've been scared of him for years.
FAITH	You, scared?
RITA	Oh yes.
FAITH	I can't believe that.
BEV	I can't.
RITA	When he loses it, believe me you wouldn't want to be in the same room.
GABBY	Has he ever hit you?
RITA	No. Been close. He once threw a saucepan at me. Fortunately I was good at netball so I caught it.

(*She tries to laugh but it turns into a sob.*)

GABBY	You sure you're okay?
RITA	Course. (*Then, near to tears.*) No. I feel so guilty. I should've taken the girls away years ago . . . but I was frightened . . . of what he'd do.

(*As* GABBY *goes to comfort her, there is a loud shattering of glass.*)

MALE VOICE	(*off*) Fucking bitch!

(*And a brick lands on the stage. As they scream, Lights out.*)

Scene Two

In the darkness we hear a mobile phone ringing. Lights up. GABBY *is sweeping up the broken glass,* BEV *drops the brick in a bin and* RITA *is just about to answer her phone.*

RITA	What the fuck do you think you're doing? (*I want you back tonight.*) No chance. You stupid get! You keep away from me, don't come near me or the girls!
	(*She switches off the phone. She's shocked, stands there.*)
BEV	What a prick!
RITA	(*upset*) He wants me to go back.
GABBY	What are you going to do?
RITA	I won't go back to him. It's taken me all this time to get away, I won't go back.
BEV	Too bloody right!
SARAH	No, you won't, Rita.
GABBY	I think we'll finish tonight. Bottle of wine on me?
	(*They all chorus 'yes'. So* GABBY *goes behind the bar, gets out a bottle of wine, starts to open it.*)
	Go and help yourselves.
	(*There's a buzz as they all help themselves to drinks.*)
SARAH	Are you worried he might be waiting for you outside?

RITA   Yeh.

GABBY   By the time we've had a few drinks he might've got fed up and gone home.

RITA   Not Terry, he's an obstinate, pig-headed bastard. He dun't really want me but he dun't want anyone else to have me either.

SARAH   Then we'll all go out together. He won't dare do anything while we're all there.

GABBY   Does he know you're staying at your Mum's?

RITA   He knows I've no where else to stay.

GABBY   Okay, well when we leave here, we'll go round to your mum's, pick up the girls and you can come and stay with me.

RITA   Oh I couldn't do that.

GABBY   Why not?

RITA   Well what if . . .

GABBY   . . . he finds us? Then we'll face him together.

RITA   You sure?

GABBY   I'm sure.

RITA   Thank you . . . just for a few days though . . .

GABBY   As long as it takes to get yourself sorted.

FAITH   Aww, that is so nice of you, Gabby.

RITA   Yeh, it is.

(GABBY *shrugs 'no problem' – as* RITA*'s mobile rings again. She picks it up.*)

RITA: It's him again.

(*She switches the mobile off completely.*)

Stuff him.

(*She raises her glass.*)

Cheers. And thanks.

BEV: How long has he been . . . ?

RITA: . . . A control freak . . . off his friggin' head? (*Shrugs.*) Dunno. He's my second husband. I was stuck in this really boring marriage . . . no passion, no sex, no conversation, dead. Then I met Terry on a girls' night out and I just like . . . totally fell for him. Slam. Left my husband in weeks . . .

SARAH: No kids with him?

RITA: Fortunately not. Moved in with Terry . . . oh wow. There was so much . . .

BEV: . . . Shagging?

RITA: Passion! Didn't know what'd hit me.

TRISHA: So when did you stop loving him?

RITA: It was 5.57 pm on Friday the 16th June 2002.

FAITH: Really? How can you be so precise?

BEV: Faith, she's taking the piss.

RITA	I don't know when I stopped loving him. It sort of creeps up on you. Maybe when we stopped laughing together and started arguing . . . or maybe when we stopped arguing and stopped talking. I don't know. But suddenly there he was, this bloke who I didn't know and who frightened the hell out of me.
FAITH	That is so sad, Rita.
RITA	(*raising her glass and knocking it back*) Mind you he did take me out for a five course meal only a month back.
FAITH	Really!
RITA	A hamburger and four cans of lager!
SARAH	At least you can laugh about it.
RITA	Yeh. (*Then more serious.*) You know . . . I look at him sitting there in front of the telly and I think, where've you gone to? 'Cos I don't know you any more. How've you changed from that guy who I worshipped to . . . (*Shrugs.*) . . .
FAITH	Aww, Rita.
RITA	. . . It's why I came here . . . I thought if I could do some pole-dancing . . . earn enough money to be like, well independent . . . I'd escape, leave him – and eventually I'd go back to nursing.
TRISHA	You were a nurse!
RITA	Yeh.
TRISHA	God, I wouldn't want you to nurse me! Did you use to swear at your patients?

RITA	Did I fuck.
SARAH	Why did you give up nursing?
RITA	Shift work. No good for bringing up kids . . . specially if your husband's a useless, lazy git.
GABBY	(*to* RITA, *holding bottle*) Another one?
RITA	Cheers.
BEV	Did you still have sex?
FAITH	Bev! That's personal!
BEV	I'm only asking. (*And she smiles at* TRISHA. *Then to* RITA.) Did you?
RITA	Yeh about three times a week.
FAITH	Three times! Well things couldn't've been . . .
RITA	But not with him. (FAITH *looks shocked.* RITA *smiles.*) Joke. Yeh, we did it occasionally. Usually when he was pissed.
BEV	Sounds familiar.
RITA	He'd get all romantic and he'd say, "Fancy a quickie?" and I'd think, "As opposed to what?"
	(*They laugh.*)
	I couldn't've said that to him though.
FAITH	Why?
RITA	He would've exploded. He lost his sense of humour . . . yet I saw him laughing in the pub with his

	mates . . . or I'd meet him from work and he'd be smiling at some of the women, his eyes all twinkly and they'd think he was a great bloke.
FAITH	That's not right, is it?
RITA	No, but I'm just the same when I'm away from him . . . laugh a minute . . . flirting like a teenager.
SARAH	So have you . . . have you . . . ?
RITA	Shagged around?
SARAH	Well I was going to say, have you had any extra-marital affairs, but yes, have you shagged around?
RITA	Oh yeh, I've shagged around.
BEV	So how many fellahs have you had . . . since you married?
RITA	First ten years . . . no one . . . then I found out Terry'd been seeing someone from work for a year.
FAITH	No!
RITA	I got this text from him – oh my lovely cherub baby, I can't wait to get my hands on your gorgeous, beautiful body. I thought, this in't like Terry. Then I realised – he'd sent it me by mistake.
FAITH	No!
GABBY	What did you do?
RITA	Sent him one back – and I can't wait to get me hands round your throat you lousy, cheating bastard!

GABBY   Oh my God.

RITA   And when he came home I told him I wanted him out – and he just crumbled . . . pathetic he was, pleaded, begged, said he'd finish with her and he was so so sorry. And I gave in . . . 'cos of the girls.

BEV   Big mistake.

RITA   Yeh. That's when I should've made the break. Instead I let him stay but never trusted him again and promptly went off and slept with this bloke from work who'd always fancied me.

BEV   Good for you.

RITA   Since then I've slept with half a dozen fellahs.

TRISHA   Half a dozen?! Good God!

FAITH   Yeh, you could've lent one to me!

(*They laugh.*)

RITA   (*to* BEV) What about you, how many fellahs have you had?

BEV   Dunno. How many baked beans in a tin? Try counting 'em, you lose track after the first fifty.

TRISHA   You've had more than fifty men?!

BEV   And if you think about it, men are a bit like baked beans. Great taste at first, but then you realise they're full of wind.

TRISHA   I can't believe you've had more than fifty men!

BEV   Probably nearer a hundred.

TRISHA	No!
SARAH	And were many of these one night stands?
BEV	Most of 'em. I've had one or two longer relationships but nothing more than a few months.
SARAH	But d'you get much satisfaction from a one night stand?
BEV	I don't let 'em go home till I do! (*She laughs.*)
SARAH	But, Bev, aren't you looking for more than just sex?
	(BEV *shrugs.*)
GABBY	Have you ever been in love, Bev?
	(BEV *is starting to get uncomfortable.*)
SARAH	Have you?
BEV	(*turning it into a joke*) What's love? Best week of your life.
SARAH	But sleeping around like that . . . does it make you happy, Bev?
BEV	You sound like a bloody psychiatrist. (*Unconvincing.*) I have a great time. I love my life. Now can we move on?
SARAH	You know, listening to you and Rita . . . I feel so naïve. The boldest thing I've ever done is come to these classes. I love my husband, but we've had a very predictable life.
RITA	You mean between the sheets?

SARAH	(*smiling*) Well that's the only place we have done it, between the sheets.
RITA	You can still have a sixty-nine in bed.
FAITH	Oh I love them. Yeh. Especially that chocolate flake in the top.
BEV	Faith, that's a ninety-nine.
SARAH	You know, Roger's the only man I've ever slept with.
	(*They respond, "No!" "Really?" apart from* FAITH.)
FAITH	That's one more than me!
SARAH	So I decided . . . I am going to experiment . . .
TRISHA	You mean experiment with other men?!
SARAH	No! Within our relationship. So today . . . I went out . . . bought some sexy underwear . . .
TRISHA	Fantastic!
SARAH	. . . And I put it on, stood in front of the mirror . . . and I did feel sexy. I'm going to surprise Roger one night.
RITA	Surprise? He'll have a bleeding heart attack!
	(*They all laugh, then* RITA *looks at* GABBY.)
	What about you, you're a bit of a dark horse, bet you got loads of offers when you were pole dancing.

GABBY	Yeh, I did. But you don't take any of them up no matter how much money they offer – and I've been offered ten grand just for one night.
	(*They all go "NO!".*)
RITA	And you didn't take it?! I bloody would've bit his bloody hand off!
GABBY	It wasn't his hand he wanted me to bite.
	(*They all laugh.*)
RITA	You must've been tempted . . . especially if it was someone good-looking, rich and charming.
	(*And* GABBY *doesn't reply.*)
	You have, haven't you?! You bloody have, you dark horse!
GABBY	No. But I did meet someone in the club once.
RITA	And what happened?
GABBY	He *was* handsome . . . rich . . . and charming. And he pursued me. He used to come to the club two or three times a week and he was only interested in me.
BEV	Sounds pervy to me.
GABBY	Yeh, you can get pervy guys, you know, who become obsessed with you . . . I mean I had one guy who wanted to buy a pair of my knickers . . .
FAITH	No!
RITA	Used?

GABBY	What d'you think?
	(*They all go "Ooooo".*)
	Anyway, he offered to give me £100 for a pair.
SARAH	Did you?
GABBY	I got the £100 off him – then I sent him a pair of my Gran's pants.
	(*They laugh.*)
	She's twenty stone, a family of twelve could camp out in them!
	(*They all laugh again.*)
	Anyway, this guy . . . he wasn't like that. He never made me feel uncomfortable. He made me laugh, he bought me expensive presents . . . which I always returned . . . and he kept asking me out. (*Beat.*) Finally I said yes.
RITA	Big mistake?
GABBY	Huge. It was after I fell in love with him that I discovered the truth . . . it was all a lie! He wasn't a rich businessman. He was unemployed. He'd only mortgaged his house, hadn't he? So he could live this . . . well I suppose, fantasy life!
FAITH	Aww, that is so awful.
GABBY	Then he went bust. Ran off with two grand of my money . . .
FAITH	No!

GABBY	Month later, found out I was pregnant.
	(*Pause. They're shocked.*)
SARAH	Have you heard from him since?
GABBY	Nothing. I managed to still carry on working here after Jay was born . . . my mum baby-sat for me overnight . . . but then I had to give it up six months ago.
SARAH	Why?
GABBY	(*looking directly at* SARAH) That's when mum died of cancer.
SARAH	Oh I'm sorry.
GABBY	Yeh. (*Still looks at* SARAH.) So . . . I have a good idea what you're going through, Sarah . . . and that's why we're going to make this charity night happen because it's important to all of us.
	(*Lights fade.*)

Scene Three

Lights up. The village hall.

SARAH *is being interviewed by a BBC Radio Interviewer. The others sit around watching, having a drink.*

SARAH	. . . And when I was diagnosed with the cancer I thought it was a really unique and novel way of raising money for cancer research.

INTERVIEWER	It's certainly that, Sarah. And I believe you've roped in all your fellow class mates to join you . . .
SARAH	Yes, they've been brilliant.

(She smiles at them, they do a thumbs up.)

INTERVIEWER	And how much money are you hoping to raise?
SARAH	Well on the night of the charity event . . . December 20th we're hoping to make at least £2,000. We're also recording a DVD of the night which will go on sale nationally where we hope to raise many thousands more. But I'm also making a DVD diary of my day to day progress. I'm having chemo but I'm also on the drug Herceptin and I want to log my progress while using it.
INTERVIEWER	And Herceptin, this is the drug that was only made available on the NHS after a lot of lobbying?
SARAH	That's right, yes.
INTERVIEWER	And I believe next month you're also planning another unusual charity event?
SARAH	Yes, I'm doing a charity bungee jump . . . from a helicopter!
INTERVIEWER	From a helicopter! Sarah, you're one very brave lady. And if anyone wants to donate to your various charity events . . .what do they have to do?
SARAH	They can log onto my website, www.sarahandfriends.com.
INTERVIEWER	That's great. I wish you all the best with it, Sarah.

(She switches off the recorder.)

	Thanks, Sarah, that was terrific.
	(*The others all clap.*)
	It'll be on *Woman's Hour* this Friday.
SARAH	Great.
INTERVIEWER	(*to all of them as she leaves*) Good luck all of you. I'm really looking forward to it.
BEV	(*after* INTERVIEWER *has exited*) I'm bloody not!
FAITH	Sarah, will the DVD of us pole dancing be an 18?
BEV	It will when they see my bloody body!
	(*As they laugh.*)
GABBY	And if you don't want to make it a comedy, we've a lot of work to do over the next few weeks. Anyway, Sarah, what's this bungee jumping?
BEV	From a friggin' helicopter!
SARAH	You see I've always been scared of heights . . . so I thought . . . do something daring . . . and raise some money . . . and the bungee jumping seemed a good idea . . . at the time.
GABBY	And now you've announced it to the world, you've got to do it.
SARAH	Exactly.
FAITH	That is so brave, Sarah.
BEV	You've more bloody balls than me!

SARAH	I hope not!
	(*They laugh.*)
RITA	Hey, I bet it's the biggest jump you've ever had!
	(*They laugh.*)
	I'll sponsor you.
	(*And they all say, "Yeh, so will I". "And me". SARAH acknowledges a "thank you" to them – as FAITH steps forward, smiling.*)
FAITH	(*quite tipsy*) I have an announcement to make actually.
RITA	You volunteer to go bungee jumping with Sarah?
FAITH	Oh no! I couldn't do that. (*Pauses, then a little smile.*) I had *my* first jump last night!
	(*They're all excited, laughing, "No!" and all at one they're asking, "Where?" "What was it like?" "Was he any good?".*)
	All right, all right . . .
RITA	Give us the gory details!
FAITH	No! (*Then she takes another drink.*) Okay! (*Pauses.*) We did it at Richie's flat, in his bedroom.
RITA	And how was it?
FAITH	Well it was . . . it was very . . . nice.
TRISHA	Very NICE?!

FAITH	Well it was okay.
RITA	Okay's not much better.
SARAH	Take no notice of them, Faith.
GABBY	Yeh, take it from me "Okay's" pretty good for a first time.
FAITH	To be honest . . . it was a bit fumbly . . .
SARAH	First time's usually are . . . mine was.
TRISHA	In what way was it fumbly, Faith?
FAITH	It was a bit like . . . you know on a fairground where you're rolling a ball into a hole and you think it's about to go in . . . then it just misses . . . well it was like that.
	(*Beat.*)
BEV	Did you win a goldfish?
	(*They laugh.*)
RITA	And did he have a big tiddler or a little tiddler?
FAITH	Rita!
	(*And they all laugh.*)
	To be honest it was all over before you could say 'big dipper'!
	(*They all laugh again*).
TRISHA	Unlike my first time with Gareth.

(*They all groan at her.*)

RITA (*mouths, mimics*) Unlike my first time with Gareth.

FAITH Anyway, I thought I'd take Bev's advice and I decided I'd bring up the subject of the clitoris.

SARAH Faith, I can't believe you were so bold!

BEV I told her every fellah should have a lesson on where the clit is.

FAITH So I said to him, Richie, d'you know the clitoris?

GABBY And what did he say to that?

FAITH He said, course I do, me dad's got some in his garden.

(*They all laugh except* FAITH *who ploughs on.*)

And I said, your dad can't grow a clitoris and he said, no, no, it was a joke, you know clitoris, clematis, and I said, well I've never heard Bev call the clitoris a clematis . . .

BEV I give up with her.

FAITH Anyway, to be honest I don't think he knew a lot about it, so I asked if he knew that the clitoris is the female equivalent of the penis and he said, 'It's a good job my penis is a bit bigger than that.'

RITA Only a bit!

FAITH He's a wonderful sense of humour you know.

RITA Oh we can tell!

FAITH	So after that we . . . we sort of experimented . . . and I . . . (*Pauses, proud.*) . . . I had an orgasm.
TRISHA	Faith!
RITA	Good on you, kid!
FAITH	And it was very, very nice . . . of course I've had them on my own . . . but it was the first time with a lad.
BEV	(*puts arm round her*) That's my mate!
RITA	And if he has trouble satisfying you in the future . . . try him on viagra.
TRISHA	I thought that was for old men who couldn't . . .
RITA	Oh no. I went with this young guy who'd taken it and it was great – at first. Then he went on and on and on and on. I fell asleep for two hours, woke up, he was still at it. I said, pull me nightie down when you've finished.
BEV	Hey, you know something . . . a big box of viagara got stolen from our local chemist recently.
RITA	Oh yeh?
BEV	The police were looking for two hardened criminals.
	(*They laugh and* RITA *nudges* BEV *at being taken in.*)
	Still, if the fellah's not up to it, you just have to rely on a girl's best friend.
FAITH	A dog?!

BEV	That's man's best friend! A vibrator!
FAITH	Ohhhh!
BEV	Reliable, faithful, doesn't fart, won't answer back and guaranteed 100% satisfaction.
RITA	Unless the batteries run out.
BEV	Hey, that happened to a mate of mine. She was desperate for an orgasm but her battery had gone – you never guess what she did? (*Beat.*) – she used her husband's electric tooth brush! |//
	(*Everyone laughs goes Noooo.*)
	She said it was a bit bristly but it did the job – (*They all laugh.*) – then she really got into it – (*Beat.*) – so she started using it regular.
	(*More laughs.*)
SARAH	Did she tell her husband?
BEV	No, did she heck. She used to watch him cleaning his teeth and he could never understand why she was killing herself laughing.
	(*They all roar with laughter. Then suddenly* RITA'S *mobile rings . . . and it brings them all down to earth.* RITA *picks it up, looks who it is and is very relieved.*)
RITA	It's okay, it's my Rosie. (*Answers it.*) Hi, Rosie. (*Mam, me dad picked us up from school.*) Where are you now? (*At our old house.*) Does your dad know you're ringing? (*Yeh, he asked me to ring.*) Put him on. (*So when you coming home.*) What d'you think you're playing at, Terry? (*I said when*

	you coming home?) I'm coming back to your place . . . to pick up the girls, but that's all, I won't be stopping. (*You will, 'cos if you don't stay I'll make the girls very happy.*) Is that a threat? Are you . . . threatening my girls? You'd better not touch them, you touch them and I'll frigging kill you!
	(*The phone goes dead. They are all looking, waiting for a response.* RITA *is near to tears, visibly shaken.*)
	He picked the girls up from school, took them back to our old house. They're scared. Rosie sounded really scared. And he's threatening me . . . if I don't go back to him, he'll harm the girls.
	(*A moment as they take this in.*)
SARAH	Right, come on! We're going round there . . . all of us. Now.
	(*Lights out.*)

Scene Four

Lights up. Village hall. They look towards RITA *as she enters from C stage entrance.*

SARAH	Are they okay?
RITA	Yeh, I've left them in the changing room, playing with their Nintendos. Anyway, thanks, guys. But specially you, Sarah, you were fantastic.
SARAH	It's amazing how brave you can be when you've nothing to lose. And I wasn't going to let him treat you like that.

FAITH	I was so scared when he threatened you, Rita.
SARAH	And I'm not sure you should've grabbed his testicles so hard, Bev.
BEV	I thought you said he was a handful!
RITA	Oh but it was lovely to see those tears in his eyes.
	(*They all laugh.*)
FAITH	Hey and fancy that taxi driver recognising you, Sarah.
SARAH	Yes, it's happening all the time.
RITA	Yeh, I got recognised by one of the mums at the school gates.
BEV	Yeh. Some bloke came up to me in the street and said, the only pole you should be swinging on is a telegraph pole – so he won't be having any more children.
	(*They laugh.*)
GABBY	Okay. We've lost an hour. Let's get down to it.
	(*She goes to pole.*)
	I'm going to show you a new move. It's not easy, but it looks good. Watch.
	(*She demonstrates.*)
BEV	You expect us to do that?
GABBY	Oh yes.

BEV	You're having a laugh, aren't you?
TRISHA	Oh I don't think that'll be a problem for me, Gabby.
RITA	(*mimicking* TRISHA) . . . Don't think that'll be a problem for me, Gabby.
GABBY	Go on, to your poles. Right, let's go for it.
	(*They try the complicated move and they are all hopeless, even* TRISHA – GABBY *starts laughing.*)
	That is so bad. Maybe we should keep that in, let the audience have a good laugh. Let's try it again.
	(*They try, not much better.*)
	If you don't get this right, forget the after session drinks. One more time.
	(*And this time they are much better.*)
	That's all the incentive you needed. Good. Let's wipe the poles.
	(*As they do a phone bleeps.*)
BEV	(*picking up mobile*) It's mine.
	(*She reads the text, starts to text back.*)
FAITH	Who's texting you, Bev?
BEV	Mind your own bloody business, Faith!
	(*And* FAITH *is a bit surprised "Oh". Then* BEV *feels bad. As she sends the text.*)
	It's just a mate.

RITA	Shag-mate or non shag-mate?
TRISHA	I think we all know the answer to that.
BEV	It's a guy I met yesterday.
FAITH	Really? You never said.
RITA	Did you drop your knickers for him?
BEV	No, I wan't wearing any!

(BEV *laughs.*)

TRISHA	That wouldn't surprise me.
FAITH	Where did you meet him, Bev?
BEV	In . . . the park . . . by the ice cream van . . . we had a sixty-nine.

(*And she smiles, points at* FAITH, *who laughs.*)

Anyway, his name's Ralph, I'm seeing him again this week and that's all I'm saying.

SARAH	Good for you, Bev. You're learning.

(SARAH *sits down, weary.*)

GABBY	You sure you're okay, Sarah?
SARAH	Just a little tired. It's the chemo. (*Pulls at hair.*) And some of my hair's started to drop out.
FAITH	Aww, Sarah.
SARAH	Anyway, got to preserve my energy 'til later this week.

RITA	Why?
SARAH	Two weeks ago I ordered . . . a pole!
	(*They all go "no".*)
	It's being delivered tomorrow.
GABBY	Sarah, you are so full of surprises!
SARAH	Roger doesn't know. They're erecting it in my bedroom.
RITA	Are they indeed? I hope it'll be the first erection of many.
	(*They all laugh. Lights out.*)

Scene Five

Lights up. The village hall. BEV *enters on her mobile.*

BEV	Yeh, I'll see you tomorrow night, same place. Okay. And you.
	(*She switches off mobile as* FAITH *follows her in.*)
FAITH	Was that Ralph?
	(BEV *nods.*)
	When am I gonna meet him?
BEV	Dunno.
FAITH	You're being very secretive about this, Bev, it's not like you.

BEV	Am I?
FAITH	Are you meeting him tonight?
BEV	Yeh.
FAITH	For a drink?
BEV	Yeh.
FAITH	Richie can't come out tonight. I'd like to meet your new guy.
BEV	Sorry.
FAITH	Why not? You've met Richie a few times now.
BEV	'Cos I want to be on me own with him. Okay?
	(FAITH *nods 'okay' again. As the others enter.*)
RITA	So did it arrive?
SARAH	(*mock ignorance*) Did what arrive?
RITA	You know what I'm talking about . . . your friggin' pole!
SARAH	Oh that. Yeh, it arrived.
	(*Sudden interest from everyone.*)
RITA	And how did Roger react when he saw it?
FAITH	Oh yeh, go on, tell us, Sarah.
SARAH	Okay, okay . . .
RITA	And don't leave out the good bits.

SARAH   All right, all right. The guy came in the morning, put it up just by the bottom of the bed . . . (*They all go "Oooo".*) . . . and when Roger came home from work . . . after dinner I told him to give me ten minutes then to come up to bed . . .

            (*They all go, "oooo" again . . . except* BEV *who has been preoccupied but now gets drawn in, smiles.*)

            When he walked in, I was standing there holding onto the pole . . . wearing a skimpy silk top . . . and a pair of crotchless knickers!

FAITH   Sarah!

TRISHA   No!

RITA   You dirty cow!

BEV   Go on!!

SARAH   He was gob-smacked.

TRISHA   I'm gob-smacked!

SARAH   And I told him to take off his clothes and lie on the bed.

FAITH   Did he?

SARAH   Did he? He couldn't rip them off fast enough!

            (*They laugh gleefully.*)

            Then I put on some sexy music and I performed for him . . . (*She stops.*)

RITA   And?

SARAH	And the rest is personal.
	(*Big groan.*)
RITA	You can't leave us like this!
BEV	Yeh, Sarah, don't be a flange!
SARAH	Let me just say this, Trisha . . . Roger didn't make love to me . . .
TRISHA	He didn't?
SARAH	He shagged me like he's never shagged me before!
	(*Cheers.*)
	It was wonderful.
	(*Cheers.*)
RITA	Well and truly rogered!
	(*They all laugh.*)
	But we had a bit of a disaster in the middle of the night.
FAITH	What?
SARAH	Roger woke up to go to the loo, forgot about the pole being there, and walked straight into it. At 4.00 am we were down at the A & E trying to explain it. He's okay though.
TRISHA	Well . . . certainly a night to remember.
FAITH	(*proud*) I did a pole dance for Richie on Wednesday night.

TRISHA   You didn't!

FAITH   Well it wasn't exactly a pole dance 'cos I didn't have a pole . . . it was more a . . .

RITA   Dance?

FAITH   Yeh. But a sexy dance. (*Beat. Provocative.*) I was very skimpily dressed!

RITA   You devil.

TRISHA   And did he like it?

FAITH   Like it! He loved it. Oh he got totally carried away, he wanted to do all sorts of stuff to me . . .

RITA   Such as?

FAITH   (*beat*) Well actually, no, he wanted me to do all sorts of stuff to him.

TRISHA   What sort of 'stuff'?

FAITH   Well, you know . . .

RITA   Like suck his dick?

FAITH   Rita! (*Then.*) Well yeh.

BEV   And did you?

FAITH   Certainly not, Bev. I think it's distasteful.

(*And they laugh at what she's said.*)

What have I said? (*Then realises.*) Ohhh.

RITA	When I used to work in a pub, this old bloke said he'd pay me a tenner to do it to him . . . I gave him a right mouthful.
	(*They laugh.*)
FAITH	Well I certainly wasn't going to do it to Richie . . . as much as I like him. How could you put a man's willy in your mouth, you don't know where it's been.
RITA	I rather like it.
FAITH	You would! You're as bad as Bev. But it's not natural, is it, Trish?
TRISHA	Actually, Faith, it's quite a turn on.
FAITH	A turn on! I'd rather chew on a Cumberland sausage!
SARAH	Or a cocktail sausage.
RITA	Anyway, you certainly don't chew!
BEV	Yeh – unless you've had an argument.
FAITH	Can we change the subject please?
BEV	Okay, we will. (*Beat.*) Has he gone down on *you* yet?
FAITH	No!
BEV	Would you like him to?
FAITH	No! . . . (*Then.*) . . . Ooo I don't know. Is it nice?
RITA	It's lovely!

BEV	'Cos if you want him to go down on you, I've got a great tip on how you can persuade him.
FAITH	How?
	(*Beat.* BEV *smiles.*)
	Go on, tells us, how?
BEV	Put his favourite food down there.
	(*And they all go "WHAT?".*)
	A mate o' mine couldn't get her boy friend to do it to her. Anyway, he loved Haagen Dazs ice cream so she smothered herself in vanilla and coffee ripple and he couldn't get down there fast enough.
	(*Throughout this they're all showing complete amazement, laughing uncontrollably.*)
	Licking away happy as a cow on his cud. She said it was lovely. Bit cold mind. He got through a whole tub and she had two orgasms.
FAITH	That's all very well, Bev, but Richie's favourite food is meat and two veg!
	(*They all laugh.*)
RITA	What if it was chicken vindaloo?
	(*They all laugh and groan at the same time.*)
FAITH	Be okay if it was toad in the hole though! Ohhh!
	(*They laugh again.* GABBY *enters.*)
GABBY	Have you done your warm-ups?

(*They all chorus, 'yes'.*)

We've got three more weeks. Show me how you've progressed. Put all the moves together you've learned.

(*She switches on the music. They start a group routine away from the poles. Again, it's not great. FAITH and BEV are still awkward. SARAH looks like she's struggling. Suddenly she collapses onto the ground. GABBY stops the music and they all rush to her. "Sarah!" "Sarah, are you okay?". They kneel down to her, try to sit her up.*)

RITA It's all that bloody shagging!

(*Lights out.*)

Scene Six

Lights up. Village hall.

Open as BEV *and the others are fixing a wig onto* SARAH *– apart from* TRISHA *who is missing. A* PHOTOGRAPHER *is waiting to take their photos.*

SARAH Make sure it's straight. What do I look like?

(*They all laugh.*)

Don't laugh.

(*And now the others step from in front of* SARAH *and we see her properly for the first time.*)

BEV (*laughing*) You look like Cilla Black! Surprise, surprise!

SARAH	Thank you.
PHOTOGRAPHER	Ready?
SARAH	Can't you wait, we've got one missing.
PHOTOGRAPHER	Sorry. Tight schedule. Okay, smile. Lovely. One more time. Thanks. That's great. See you, and good luck.
	(*He exits.*)
BEV	Wonder if they'll put us on Page Three?
RITA	If I'd known that I would've got me tits out.
	(*Now the others all separate from the podium and for the first time we see* SARAH *is sitting down. She hauls herself out of the chair with some difficulty.*)
SARAH	What d'you think's happened to Trisha?
GABBY	Anyway, we can't wait for her. Let's get started. (*Looking at* SARAH.) I think you should sit this out.
SARAH	Don't you start, Gabby. Roger's already wrapping me in cotton wool, treating me like some invalid. I'm not, I'm just a little tired and the chemo's making me feel sick but apart from that I'm terrific.
GABBY	I really don't think you should be doing this.
SARAH	I have to do it, we've only got two weeks before the charity.
GABBY	I think you need to take another week off.
SARAH	I can't. I've already missed one week! I miss a second week and we're not going to be ready.

(*The others are looking closely at her.*).

You don't think I'm going to make it, do you?

(*A moment. No, they don't.*)

FAITH Yes! Course we do.

(*And the others join in unconvincingly.*)

SARAH You're wrong. Well I am. And I'm determined to perform at the charity, no matter what . . . and believe me I'm not going to die – well not yet.

(*Beat.*)

GABBY Well that told us. Okay, let's warm up.

(*As they are about to start,* BEV *puts up her hand.*)

BEV Please, Miss, can I go for a poo.

(GABBY *nods.* BEV *exits.*)

GABBY Where the hell is Trisha?

FAITH It's not like Trish to be late, she's always very punctuated.

GABBY And punctual.

RITA I saw you on *Newsnight* last night.

FAITH Oh you were very good, Sarah.

RITA And what's he like that Jeremy Paxman?

SARAH Very nice actually.

RITA	Did you shag him?
SARAH	Only twice.
FAITH	Sarah! You didn't?!! (*And she realises from the reactions of the others she's been duped.*). Ohhh.
SARAH	Actually he really was very nice – well to me he was. And off camera everyone was fussing round me like I was royalty. It's like, suddenly I've got this great power. People will do anything for me, they don't want to upset me, they want to make me happy.
FAITH	Aww, Sarah . . .
RITA	And how you feeling now?
SARAH	Oh, you know . . . up and down.
RITA	So you are still having sex then.
GABBY	(*as* TRISHA *enters*) Trisha, you're late.
	(*She looks distraught. They pick up on it.*)
SARAH	Everything all right, Trisha?
	(TRISHA *shakes her head.*)
GABBY	What is it?
	(TRISHA *shakes her head, won't tell them.*)
SARAH	Come on, Trisha . . . it can't be that bad.
	(TRISHA *nods her head. "It is".*)
	Tell us, Trisha, you're amongst friends.

(*A moment then* TRISHA *bursts in tears, big, huge sobs.*)

TRISHA Gareth's having an affair!

(*And she bursts into even greater sobbing. There's total disbelief from everyone.* "No", "Gareth?" "No way".)

SARAH How d'you know he's having an affair?

TRISHA I know.

GABBY Has he told you?

TRISHA No.

RITA So how d'you know?

SARAH Have you spoken to him about it?

TRISHA No.

SARAH So how can you be sure?

FAITH Yeh, Gareth wouldn't have an affair, he's too nice.

TRISHA He's been working late a lot recently . . . so one night I rang him at work . . . and he wasn't there.

SARAH Didn't you ask him where he was when he got home?

TRISHA (*nods*) He said he'd gone for a drink with his mates from work . . .

FAITH Well then . . .

TRISHA He never goes for a drink with his work mates . . .

FAITH	He might have . . .
TRISHA	He doesn't like his work mates . . . so I got suspicious . . . and when he was out I started looking through his things and stuff . . .
RITA	What stuff?
TRISHA	Like his credit card statement . . . and he's paid for meals when he was supposed to be working . . . and then . . . (*Pauses.*)
RITA	What?
TRISHA	(*taking scrap of paper from her bag*) I found this phone number rolled up, hidden, in the back pocket of his trousers . . .
GABBY	Could be nothing.
	(*A moment.*)
SARAH	Have you tried ringing it?
TRISHA	No. I'm scared. What would I say? What if I'm wrong? What if it's a fellah?
RITA	You think Gareth might be gay?!
TRISHA	No! Of course he's not gay! I mean . . . if it's a mate's number.
RITA	There's only one way to find out.
	(*Beat.* TRISHA *takes out her phone, is about to ring, pauses.*)
TRISHA	Sarah, will you ring it for me?

SARAH	What will I say?
TRISHA	You'll know what to say, you always do. (*Beat.*) Please?
	(*A moment.* SARAH *nods and takes the phone and number. She starts to dial. Everyone waits in anticipation – when suddenly a phone starts ringing on stage. They're all shocked, amazed. They look where the ringing's coming from. A bag.* BEV *enters, goes across to the bag.*)
BEV	Hey guys, why didn't one of you answer it.
	(*She takes out her phone . . .*)
	Hi.
SARAH	Hello, Bev.
	(*They're all stunned.* BEV *is confused.*)
BEV	Sarah? Why you ringing me?
FAITH	I don't understand it.
TRISHA	(*confused*) No. I mean . . . what's going on?
BEV	Yeh, what the frigging hell is going on?
TRISHA	Why's Gareth got your phone number . . . ?
BEV	What?
TRISHA	I found your number in his back pocket. Why's he got it?
	(*No answer from* BEV.)

SARAH	There must be a simple explanation, Bev.
FAITH	Yeh, course there must.
	(*A moment.*)
TRISHA	Well?
	(BEV *is in a huge dilemma.*)
GABBY	We're all waiting, Bev.
BEV	(*eventually*) Yeh, there is. There is an explanation.
FAITH	See!
TRISHA	So what is it?
	(*Beat.*)
BEV	I've . . . I've been seeing Gareth.
RITA	Fuck me!
	(*A moment for* TRISHA *to take this in. Then* TRISHA *laughs.*)
TRISHA	Oh yes, very funny, well I don't find it at all funny, I think it's sick!
SARAH	Bev, if this is a joke, it's not very . . .
BEV	It's no joke.
FAITH	Course it's a joke, it's Ralph she's been seeing . . . (*Pauses.*)
BEV	There is no Ralph.

GABBY	Oh dear.
	(*Stunned silence. Eventually* TRISHA *responds.*)
TRISHA	No! No, I don't believe it . . .
BEV	I'm sorry . . .
TRISHA	Gareth wouldn't have an affair with you, he just wouldn't!
BEV	Why not?
TRISHA	Well, just . . . just look at you . . . you're like . . . you're like a beached whale!
BEV	Gareth prefers bigger women.
TRISHA	What?
BEV	He always has.
TRISHA	Gareth prefers bigger women?
BEV	He never wanted you to lose all that weight.
TRISHA	Of course he did!
BEV	He tried to tell you but you wouldn't listen.
TRISHA	You're talking rubbish, Gareth likes thin, slender women!
BEV	He doesn't.
TRISHA	I don't believe you. You're winding me up, aren't you?
SARAH	I don't think she is, Trisha.

BEV	. . . And I'm so sorry . . .
TRISHA	. . . You hardly know each other!
BEV	We've been seeing each other since your party.
TRISHA	Our party! Our anniversary party!
BEV	I love him, Trisha . . . and Gareth . . . he loves me.
TRISHA	Gareth says he loves you? (BEV *nods.*) How could he love you, you, you of all people . . . you're . . . you're crude and foul-mouthed and . . . !
BEV	He finds me funny. I make him laugh. Something you've not done for . . . (*Shrugs.*)
TRISHA	(*crying*) I thought you were my friend!
BEV	I am, I . . .
TRISHA	Friend?! Friend!! Don't you call yourself a friend!!
BEV	I tried to stop it but . . .
TRISHA	You are not my friend!
BEV	I haven't slept with him.
	(*Which stops* TRISHA *in her tracks.*)
	I haven't.
TRISHA	You expect me to believe that? You of all people!
BEV	I didn't want to hurt you . . . and I . . . I didn't want to spoil it for me and Gareth . . . you know something . . . I have never loved anyone before and . . .

TRISHA	Bitch!
BEV	Trisha, you got so obsessed with losing weight, Gareth couldn't get through to you . . .
TRISHA	. . . Bitch
BEV	. . . and he said it changed you . . . your personality . . . it was like he didn't know you.

(*Now* TRISHA *snaps. She breaks down into an angry, sobbing wail and rushes at* BEV, *starts to hit her and* BEV *just takes it.*)

TRISHA	You bitch! You bitch . . . you evil, fucking bitch!

(*Then still hysterical she runs out. Silence. The four of them look at* BEV. RITA, *who has actually been quite enjoying this smiles.*)

RITA	(*gleeful*) What a fucking turn up! Not happy, is she?
SARAH	Rita, please!
RITA	Sorry – but it is bloody funny.
GABBY	Not for Trisha.
SARAH	(*turns to* BEV) How could you, Bev?
BEV	I couldn't help it.
RITA	That's what fellahs say.

(BEV *shrugs, "I know".*)

FAITH	Oh Bev . . . I can't believe . . . I mean . . . you and Gareth . . .

(BEV *shrugs again.*)

BEV (*to* SARAH) You asked me if I'd ever been in love. I laughed it off. But you know, I never had . . . before I met Gareth.

SARAH I know.

BEV And all those men I went with . . . none of them . . . not one of them meant anything . . .

SARAH So why did you sleep with them?

BEV (*shrugs*) Made me feel in control. I was like a man. (*Pauses.*) But you know the loneliest moment in the whole world? It's a one night stand after you've had sex and he turns over and goes to sleep – or worse, gets dressed and goes home. Those moments, I sometimes cry. Just to myself. And in the morning . . . you can't even remember his name

(BEV *fills up.* SARAH *now feels sorry for her. She goes to her, gives her a hug.*)

You know Gareth and me . . . we really haven't had sex.

RITA You must be straining at the lead like a couple o' rampant dogs!

SARAH Rita . . .

GABBY Shame it had to be Trisha's husband you fell in love with.

BEV Yeh. I felt so guilty . . . I like Trisha . . . she's a pain in the arse but I like her.

SARAH	And d'you really think it's going to work out between you and Gareth?
BEV	(*smiles*) Yeh. Hope so. He makes me happy. I make him happy. And he made me realise how unhappy I'd been.
RITA	Tell you what though . . . I'd love to be a fly on the wall when she gets home to *her* Gareth tonight!

(*Lights out.*)

Scene Seven

Lights up. The village hall.

BEV *and* FAITH *enter. They dance and mime actions to "It's Raining Men". After they've finished.*

FAITH	Oh Bev, I'm so nervous. (*Hold out her arm, her fingers are shaking.*) Look. Are you?
BEV	Just try and enjoy it.
FAITH	Enjoy it! I don't even know if I can go through with it.
	(FAITH *moves to leave.*)
BEV	Faith, Faith, come on, come on!
	(*And* BEV *points for her to get on the podium.* FAITH *steps onto it.*)
FAITH	How's Gareth by the way . . . since Trisha broke his nose.

BEV   Not too good – specially as he's got hay fever.

FAITH   Oh dear. Seen Trisha?

BEV   Not since Gareth moved in with me.

FAITH   No, she's not been in touch with me . . . God, I really am nervous.

(*As* GABBY *breezes in.*)

GABBY   Have you seen the queue outside . . .

FAITH   Queue?!

GABBY   . . . It's amazing. Right round the block.

FAITH   Oh my God!

GABBY   Never seen anything like it. Even TV cameras out there. Hope everyone can get in.

FAITH   I wish I'd never said yes to this.

(FAITH *fishes in her bag, takes out some sandwiches.*)

GABBY   It's in a good cause, Faith.

FAITH   I know . . . but I'm still wetting meself.

(*Offering a sandwich.*)

Would you like a ham and peanut butter sandwich?

GABBY   (*taking them off her*) Thanks.

FAITH   What are you doing?

GABBY	(*as she throws them in the bin*) You and your bloody sandwiches! D'you want to be sick on stage?
FAITH	I don't even want to go on stage!
	(*As* RITA *enters. They all say hi.*)
RITA	Bad news.
BEV	What?
RITA	I mean, bad bad news.
	(*They're waiting for a response.*)
	Had a call from Roger this afternoon . . . Sarah's been rushed into hospital.
FAITH	Oh no, how is she?
RITA	Not good. Really not good.
BEV	Oh shit.
	(*Pause as they take this in. They are very upset.*)
FAITH	What are we going to do?
GABBY	I don't know.
FAITH	We can't go on without Sarah.
GABBY	And what about Trisha? Has anyone heard from her?
BEV	She's not gonna turn up, is she? I mean, would you?

RITA — Thanks a bunch, Bev.

BEV — Yeh, I know, I fucked it up . . . sorry.

FAITH — So there's just the three of us?

GABBY — Looks like it.

BEV — We'll have to cancel.

RITA — What about all the people outside?

(*They think about this too.*)

FAITH — I'm not going on with just the three of us.

(*And unseen,* TRISHA *has entered.*)

TRISHA — Who says it'll be just the three of you.

FAITH — Trisha!

RITA — We didn't think you'd turn up.

TRISHA — No? (*Looking at* BEV.) I may have lost my husband . . . but I haven't lost my dignity. And I won't let Sarah down.

FAITH — Trisha, Sarah's in hospital. She's not going to be here . . . in fact she's really really . . .

(*And* FAITH *feel overwhelmed and starts crying.*)

TRISHA — You're not thinking of cancelling?

FAITH — (*still crying*) But Sarah's not going to be here.

TRISHA	Would Sarah want us to cancel?
	(*A moment, they all agree she wouldn't. "No", "No, she wouldn't".*)
TRISHA	Of course she wouldn't. So we go on. We do it for Sarah. Yeh?
	(*A moment. They all agree.*)
GABBY	Okay, ladies, go and get changed, I'll open the doors and introduce you. And good luck.
	(*They exit.* BEV *and* TRISHA *find themselves face to face.*)
BEV	I really am sorry, Trish, what's happened, what I've done to you . . .
TRISHA	(*proud*) You know something, Bev, I was so scared of losing Gareth . . . and so *grateful* he married me. But you know, now I have lost him, it's nowhere near as frightening as I thought it would be. I'll survive . . . and you know why? Because I am totally, irresistibly gorgeous!
	(*And she turns, flouts away. Lights fade.*)

Scene Eight

Spot up on GABBY.

GABBY	And that's our story. All six months of it. We've laughed, we've cried, we've shared some very personal stories and along the way we've had some fantastic times. And tonight was meant to be very special. But I'm afraid I've got some sad news for

	you. Earlier today Sarah was taken into hospital and unfortunately she won't be here tonight.

(*But suddenly* SARAH *enters unsteadily.*)

SARAH	Oh yes she will.
GABBY	Sarah! I thought you were in hospital.
SARAH	Discharged myself. I'm going to miss my own funeral, d'you really think I'm going to miss this? So carry on, Gabby . . .
GABBY	Are you sure? Are you sure you're . . . (*up to it*)?
SARAH	Never felt better!

(*And with that she exits.* GABBY *is thrown for a second, then she smiles.*)

GABBY Okay, let's do as the lady says . . . let's get on with the show . . . so this . . . this, ladies and gentleman, is what you've all been waiting for . . . thank you all for coming on this very special night and thank you for supporting this very special cause. And first up we have two lovely ladies . . . here they are . . . a big hand for . . . Bev and Faith.

(*Spot out. Lights up.* BEV *and* FAITH *are at a pole each. They are wearing outrageous, over-the-top, very garish, bright costumes. Music starts. However, they don't do a traditional pole dance, they do a purposely comic routine that is funky, funny, quirkily hilarious, sometimes dancing with each other. They finish. Lights out.*)

(*Lights up and* GABBY *performs a pole dance. Lights out.*)

(*Lights up.* RITA *does a pole dance. Lights out.*)

(*Lights up.* TRISHA *does a pole dance. Lights out.*)

(*Spot up on* GABBY.)

GABBY   Now please give a hand for one very, very brave lady.

(SARAH *enters slowly, unsteadily. The music starts. A slow number. She does a move then suddenly slips. The music stops as* GABBY *runs on.*)

GABBY   Sarah, are you . . . ?

SARAH   I'm fine . . . I'm fine.

(GABBY *pauses but then retreats off stage as* SARAH *stands and continues her routine from where she left off. At the end of the routine, lights out.*)

(*Lights up as all the women enter and perform a group dance/routine to "Sisters Are Doing It For Themselves". At the end of the routine they all bow. Lights out.*)

(*Lights up for a final bow and encore routine. The end.*)